Future Teaching Roles
for Academic Librarians

Future Teaching Roles for Academic Librarians has been co-published simultaneously as *College & Undergraduate Libraries,* Volume 6, Number 2 2000.

The *College & Undergraduate Libraries* Monographic "Separates"

Below is a list of "separates," which in serials librarianship means a special issue simultaneously published as a special journal issue or double-issue *and* as a "separate" hardbound monograph. (This is a format which we also call a "DocuSerial.")

"Separates" are published because specialized libraries or professionals may wish to purchase a specific thematic issue by itself in a format which can be separately cataloged and shelved, as opposed to purchasing the journal on an on-going basis. Faculty members may also more easily consider a "separate" for classroom adoption.

"Separates" are carefully classified separately with the major book jobbers so that the journal tie-in can be noted on new book order slips to avoid duplicate purchasing.

You may wish to visit Haworth's website at . . .

http://www.haworthpressinc.com

. . . to search our online catalog for complete tables of contents of these separates and related publications.

You may also call 1-800-HAWORTH (outside US/Canada: 607-722-5857), or Fax 1-800-895-0582 (outside US/Canada: 607-771-0012), or e-mail at:

getinfo@haworthpressinc.com

Future Teaching Roles for Academic Librarians, edited by Alice Harrison Bahr, PhD (Vol. 6, No. 2, 2000). *This vital guide examines current methods and suggestions on how to teach new technological developments to give patrons essential services and information.*

Future Teaching Roles for Academic Librarians

Alice Harrison Bahr, PhD
Editor

Future Teaching Roles for Academic Librarians has been co-published simultaneously as *College & Undergraduate Libraries,* Volume 6, Number 2 2000.

The Haworth Press, Inc.
New York · London · Oxford

Published by

The Haworth Press, Inc., 10 Alice Street, Binghamton, NY 13904-1580 USA

Future Teaching Roles for Academic Librarians has been co-published simultaneously as *College & Undergraduate Libraries*, Volume 6, Number 2 2000.

The development, preparation, and publication of this work has been undertaken with great care. However, the publisher, employees, editors, and agents of The Haworth Press and all imprints of The Haworth Press, Inc., including The Haworth Medical Press® and Pharmaceutical Products Press®, are not responsible for any errors contained herein or for consequences that may ensue from use of materials or information contained in this work. Opinions expressed by the author(s) are not necessarily those of The Haworth Press, Inc.

Cover design by Thomas J. Mayshock Jr.

Library of Congress Cataloging-in-Publication Data

Future teaching roles for academic librarians / Alice Harrison Bahr, editor.
    p. cm.
    Published also as v. 6, no. 2, 2000 of College & undergraduate libraries.
    Includes bibliographical references and index.
    ISBN 0-7890-0974-9 (alk. paper) -- ISBN 0-7890-0992-7 (pbk. : alk. paper)
    1. Library orientation for college students--United States. I. Bahr, Alice Harrison.

Z711.2 .F87 2000
027.6'2--dc21

                00-021101

INDEXING & ABSTRACTING

Contributions to this publication are selectively indexed or abstracted in print, electronic, online, or CD-ROM version(s) of the reference tools and information services listed below. This list is current as of the copyright date of this publication. See the end of this section for additional notes.

- *BUBL Information Service: An Internet-based Information Service for the UK higher education community <URL: http://bubl.ac.uk/>*
- *Children's Literature Abstracts*
- *CNPIEC Reference Guide: Chinese National Directory of Foreign Periodicals*
- *Current Index to Journals in Education*
- *Educational Administration Abstracts (EAA)*
- *FINDEX <www.publist.com>*
- *Higher Education Abstracts*
- *IBZ International Bibliography of Periodical Literature*
- *Index to Periodical Articles Related to Law*
- *Information Reports & Bibliographies*
- *Information Science Abstracts*
- *Informed Librarian, The. For more information visit us at: <http://infosourcespub.com>*
- *INSPEC*
- *Journal of Academic Librarianship: Guide to Professional Literature, The*
- *Konyvtari Figyelo-Library Review*
- *Library and Information Science Annual (LISCA). Further information is available at <www.lu.com/arba>*
- *Library & Information Science Abstracts (LISA)*
- *Library Digest*
- *Library Literature*

(continued)

- *Newsletter of Library and Information Services*
- *Operations Research/Management Science*
- *PAIS (Public Affairs Information Service) NYC <www.pais.org>*
- *Referativnyi Zhurnal (Abstracts Journal of the All-Russian Institute of Scientific and Technical Information)*
- *Sociological Abstracts (SA) <www.csa.com>*

Special Bibliographic Notes related to special journal issues (separates) and indexing/abstracting:

- indexing/abstracting services in this list will also cover material in any "separate" that is co-published simultaneously with Haworth's special thematic journal issue or DocuSerial. Indexing/abstracting usually covers material at the article/chapter level.
- monographic co-editions are intended for either non-subscribers or libraries which intend to purchase a second copy for their circulating collections.
- monographic co-editions are reported to all jobbers/wholesalers/approval plans. The source journal is listed as the "series" to assist the prevention of duplicate purchasing in the same manner utilized for books-in-series.
- to facilitate user/access services all indexing/abstracting services are encouraged to utilize the co-indexing entry note indicated at the bottom of the first page of each article/chapter/contribution.
- this is intended to assist a library user of any reference tool (whether print, electronic, online, or CD-ROM) to locate the monographic version if the library has purchased this version but not a subscription to the source journal.
- individual articles/chapters in any Haworth publication are also available through the Haworth Document Delivery Service (HDDS).

Future Teaching Roles for Academic Librarians

CONTENTS

ABOUT THE EDITOR

Alice Harrison Bahr, PhD, Director of the Library at Spring Hill College (Mobile, AL), earned a MLS in 1972 and a MA and PhD in English Literature in 1975 and 1980, respectively. As a practicing college librarian for more than twenty-five years, she has written several monographs and has contributed articles to the *Encyclopedia of Library and Information Service, College & Research Libraries, Government Publications Review,* and *Library Trends.* She was founding editor of *College & Undergraduate Libraries* from 1994 through 1999. Currently, she chairs the Research for College Librarianship Committee of the College Library Section of the Association of College and Research Libraries of the American Library Association.

Introduction

Alice Harrison Bahr

With the new millennium upon us and decades of discussion about change in higher education both behind us and continuing, a dialogue among educators, administrators, accreditors, and librarians about these changes and their effect on libraries, particularly their effect on librarians' instructional programs and instructional roles seems appropriate. The new paradigm for higher education involves a dramatic shift from passive teaching to interactive, collaborative student-centered learning, not of facts, but of processes that help learners think critically and apply concepts creatively. The library is critical to this shift.

Contributors to this volume signal the central role libraries can play in effecting change in higher education:

> Current attention to student learning represents a genuine opportunity to redefine relations between librarians and faculty. . . . James Wilkinson (Director of Harvard University's Derek Bok Center for Teaching and Learning)

> The usual educational division of labor, confining the librarians to the retrieval of the resources and the course instructor to the pedagogical use of those resources just won't work. George Allan (Professor Emeritus at Dickinson College)

> . . . educational change and reform are tools for academic librarians to begin building learning libraries. Kimberley M. Donnelly (Reference Librarian at York College of Pennsylvania)

Alice Harrison Bahr (PhD, Lehigh University; MLS, Drexel University) is Director of the Library, Spring Hill College, Mobile, AL 36608, and was Editor of *College & Undergraduate Libraries* from 1994 through 1999 (address e-mail to: bahr@aza lea.shc.edu).

[Haworth co-indexing entry note]: "Introduction." Bahr, Alice Harrison. Co-published simultaneously in *College & Undergraduate Libraries* (The Haworth Press, Inc.) Vol. 6, No. 2, 2000, pp. 1-4; and: *Future Teaching Roles for Academic Librarians* (ed: Alice Harrison Bahr) The Haworth Press, Inc., 2000, pp. 1-4. Single or multiple copies of this article are available for a fee from The Haworth Document Delivery Service [1-800-342-9678, 9:00 a.m. - 5:00 p.m. (EST). E-mail address: getinfo@haworthpressinc.com].

Perhaps the answer to the question of how librarians should describe their instructional programming is to shift the focus from a single descriptive label to a learning environment adept at providing a range of skills along a spectrum bounded by surface and deep learning. For lack of a better term call it a learning library, which is really not a physical entity at all but a process. . . . Steven J. Bell (Library Director at Philadelphia University)

. . . the most effective librarians in the new millennium will be those who empower learners and who facilitate the teaching and learning process. Howard L. Simmons (Professor, Educational Leadership and Policy Studies, Arizona State University)

The single most important step that academic librarians can take right now is to help faculty find ways to develop curriculum bridges from the natural critical nature of students to the formal contextual judgments they must make in any specific subject discipline. . . . If there are important questions that beg for answers before librarians can redefine the teaching role of libraries, librarians have . . . never been in a stronger position . . . to engage in the research necessary for meaningful solutions. Barbara MacAdam (Head of Educational and Information Services at the University of Michigan Library)

These authors also offer concrete, practical ways to reform traditional library instructional programs in the context of change. Recognizing that learning often deepens as part of a conversation with someone more experienced in the search for knowledge, George Allan suggests that librarians serve as critics, mentors, and role models to their learning communities. Instead of engaging students only at the beginning of an assignment, why not engage them in discussions about their choices of resources during brief, early-in-the-semester oral presentations? Then, follow that with a subsequent assignment, fashioning a dialogue, helping students learn by doing rather than by prescribing right rules of action.

James Wilkinson envisions librarians offering coffee conferences for faculty, providing opportunities to discuss new or little known collections and resources for the purpose of investigating how these resources might generate assignments that fit into a college's articulated information literacy design and objectives or, on a less grand scale, into an instructor's learning context for a course. Steven J. Bell explores programs offering in-time assistance that stretch the traditional concept of Reference Desk assistance, such as training student residence hall directors to help other students with research and connecting to students in labs when and where they're struggling to understand what databases to use or how to use them.

For Kimberley Donnelly, who surveys several options for serving students' learning needs, the success of creating a learning library rests less on any specific approach than on an organization-wide commitment evidenced by, "the creation of unified competencies throughout the curriculum. . . ." Taking the discussion one step further, Barbara MacAdam argues that librarians are in no position to discuss transforming libraries on any level without questioning the premises on which traditional library instruction rests: that the librarian's job is to prescribe the right courses of action, regardless of student preferences and values.

Despite the different approaches that the writers in this volume take to examine new teaching roles for librarians, they share a set of beliefs:

- that the new paradigm for higher education reflects a need to focus on learning, not teaching;
- that the new learning-centered focus of higher education prizes the importance of learning by doing; and
- that in this new environment, librarians have new opportunities to play a forceful, dynamic role in collaboratively designing and developing the contexts for learning strategies.

Basically, the contributors suggest that librarians should do what administrators are now asking faculty to do: see the whole picture in a larger context than ever before. This is the same charge issued early on by one of the most influential voices in educational change and the opportunities it affords librarians to help restructure the teaching/ learning process. In speaking about the changing educational climate, Patricia Senn Breivik notes that it "will also allow us to make a more profound impact on education *if* we are willing to move beyond current programs to becoming involved with restructuring efforts and use our influence and expertise to support resource-based learning with a goal of creating lifelong learners who are so because they are information literate (Breivik, 1989, 3).

In viewing the larger picture, the language of education becomes blurred and confusing. Consequently, some of the writers in this work side-step issues of language, others focus on theory, and others wrestle with terminology in an attempt to bring the angel down. Ultimately, however, as Steven J. Bell says, "Those are merely labels." What matters is that librarians shed their preconceptions about their roles, what students need, and how faculty, librarians, and other campus members should collaborate and share responsibility for teaching and learning. Even the tried and true course-related bibliographic instruction–which works–would improve, wedded to a more holistic vision of college-wide, discipline-specific objectives for information literacy. As Allan says so beautifully, learning rests on a difficult art: creating "contexts for learning" that, like a spider's web, are "fine enough to catch the prey she seeks, coarse enough to let through the insects she has no interest in, [and] flexible enough to bend with the wind. . . ."

REFERENCE

Breivik, Patricia Senn, "Information Literacy: Revolution in Education." In *Coping with Information Illiteracy: Bibliographic Instruction for the Information Age*. Eds. Glenn E. Mensching, Jr. and Teresa B. Mensching. Ann Arbor, Michigan: Pierian Press, 1989: 1-6.

The Art of Learning with Difficulty

George Allan

SUMMARY. Librarians should be actively involved in educating students: not merely teaching them the techniques needed for bibliographic searches, but helping them learn the artistry involved in thinking for themselves. This is not a matter of expertise, of teaching rules for use in academic specialties. It's a matter of creating interactive contexts–conversations–in which students can acquire by experience the general good sense needed to be able to decide in situations, specialized or not, which rules to use and why. *[Article copies available for a fee from The Haworth Document Delivery Service: 1-800-342-9678. E-mail address: getinfo@haworth pressinc.com <Website: http://www.haworthpressinc.com>]*

KEYWORDS. Teaching, learning, technique, artistry, rules, rule sorters, good sense, conversation, librarian as generalist, Rousseau, Dewey, Aristotle

What would you have him think about, when you do all the thinking for him?

–Rousseau

Rousseau's 18th century question from *Emile* strikes me as a fitting epigraph for a 21st century topic. Our question is: how can librarians best contribute to the education of young people? Rousseau's answer:

George Allan (PhD, Yale University) is Professor of Philosophy Emeritus at Dickinson College, where he was also senior academic officer from 1974-1996.

Address correspondence to: George Allan, PhD, 238 West South Street, Carlisle, PA 17013-2824 (address e-mail to: allang@kns.net).

[Haworth co-indexing entry note]: "The Art of Learning with Difficulty." Allan, George. Co-published simultaneously in *College & Undergraduate Libraries* (The Haworth Press, Inc.) Vol. 6, No. 2, 2000, pp. 5-23; and: *Future Teaching Roles for Academic Librarians* (ed: Alice Harrison Bahr) The Haworth Press, Inc., 2000, pp. 5-23. Single or multiple copies of this article are available for a fee from The Haworth Document Delivery Service [1-800-342-9678, 9:00 a.m. - 5:00 p.m. (EST). E-mail address: getinfo@haworth pressinc.com].

by helping them learn to think for themselves, rather than trying to do their thinking for them. Or if you prefer the current buzz words to Rousseau's: by empowering students, by creating student-centered learning opportunities, by deploying interactive learning pedagogies. You knew that already, of course. Your real concern is with a different question: how are librarians to contribute to this age-old task in the new age upon us, this high tech information age with its global village and world economy? What can librarians, recently become Information Specialists at Information Resource Centers, do so that students will be able to think for themselves? And, I would presume you hasten to add, so that in doing so they will have something worthwhile to think about?

The answer to these questions would seem to be straightforward. Librarians should be organizing ways to introduce students to on-line catalogs, CD-ROMs, Internet webcrawlers, information retrieval search engines on specialized data bases, newsgroups, on-line journals and magazines, e-mail with buddy pop-ups, and so forth. Librarians should be showing students how they can gain access to texts, hyper-texts, webtexts, still images, dynamic images, sounds, data bundles, and just about any other conceivable information form, no matter where it might happen to be physically located. With these resources ready at hand, supplemented by wired classrooms and interactive video, students will be properly equipped to participate fully in the paper-less classrooms that will be the signature learning environments of the new century. More likely and better yet, what they will be poised to become is denizens of classless classrooms and consumers of teacher-less teaching.

In a high tech library designed to support this sort of high tech learning, the librarian's primary task will no longer be–already is no longer–a matter of acquiring, cataloging, and managing information in the form of paper or celluloid artifacts stored in a brick-and-mortar warehouse. The librarian's base of operations will no longer be a physical location, a building or set of buildings somewhere on campus in which are kept the resources comprising all or nearly all the materials students need in order to pursue their education and faculty their scholarship. For as these materials are increasingly becoming electronic, the location of the warehouse is becoming irrelevant. There is little need anymore for a college or university to store anything, even electronically, except what has been created by its own faculty and students. O brave new world, with such libraries in't!

The main thing left for librarians to do, it would seem, is to instruct neophytes in how to use electronic access tools and to assist advanced students who have technical questions about the ins and outs of the more sophisticated of those tools. And, of course, someone still has to supervise and occasionally even help those who shelve the books and periodicals that remain as our reminder of a pre-tech heritage. But librarians who might be content with this kind of role will find their satisfaction short-lived. Query-oriented "smart" information retrieval systems are already dispensing with the need for tools of instruction, and either robots will eventually do both the supervising and the shelving or retrospective scanning will eliminate the relevance of the paper book for any purpose except those of antiquarian collectors.

From the state of affairs deplored by Rousseau, where you were doing "all the thinking" for the student patron, technology has brought you to the threshold of a state of affairs where you will be doing none of it. In the twinkling of an eye, perhaps no more than again the time it has taken to get from punchcards to now, librarians can expect to join the ranks of the structurally unemployed. Unless, if you happen to be tenured, the administration might see its way to having you retrained as a computer technician or an admissions counselor.

Yet even if you aren't the target of a retrenchment mandate, is this really what you want? Will genuine learning really be going on in this scenario of the 21st century library that I've been sketching? My answer to both questions is negative: this is not really the way we want our high tech libraries to function, and it isn't because in such a context learning will not really go on. My little story of new-age librarians at work focused completely on process. I envisioned them teaching students how to use the best of the cutting-edge information retrieval tools, how to acquire information from all possible sources in all possible formats and kinds, and how to do all of this with mind-bending alacrity. Not a word was said about content.

Okay, so what about content? Surely we don't suppose that students should actually read (listen to, see, interact with) the stuff they re-trieve. Can we really expect them to be doing something with all this information they collect? Like thinking about it. Like imagining new forms of it and linkages among its disparate elements. Like proposing, inventing, testing its implications. Perhaps even ending up with results that increase in some small way the amount of information others will need to access and acquire. Yes, of course content is more important than the process of acquiring it. Learning the content of an information search–studying it, digesting it, enjoying it, utilizing it–is the whole point of the process.

You'll be delighted to know, however, that I'm not about to inscribe the device of content on my shield and go charging off into the culture wars. I have no flag to fly in the service of Great Books, core courses, basic education, acquisitions policies, optimal collection development, and other matters of canon. Nor will I break a lance on behalf of a multicultural enlargement or radical deconstruction of any canon, so as to give voice to the voiceless or to undermine the conditions for marginalization as such. These wars very much needed to have been waged, even though the ravages of battle were often more horrifying than edifying. Right now, however, a reconciling peace needs desperately to be waged instead. But that's not my aim here.

I want to talk about process rather than content, but process in a different sense than what has so far been mentioned. I want to call attention to the adverbial aspect of a process rather than the verbal, and to argue that to know how to go about learning things is far more important for students than what it is they've learned. The "how," after all, can get you the "what" whenever you need it. Or as John Dewey puts it: "To find out how to make knowledge when it is needed is the true end of the acquisition of information in school, not the information itself" (Dewey, 221). I quote him partly because this is an essay about education and Dewey sits at the right hand of Socrates in the educational pantheon. But I also quote Dewey to remind us, since his words were written in 1915, that the current educational innovations behind the buzz words mentioned at the start of this essay are not so much innovations as reappropriations. Dewey, as always, was there first and more profoundly.

The true purpose in learning how to acquire information, says Dewey, is not the information but the acquiring. It's not enough, however, to know how to acquire knowledge in some abstract sense. We need to know how to acquire it when needed. Dewey's "when needed" qualifier is crucial: he thinks it important to be able to determine when knowledge is needed and when it's not. This ability implies, in turn, being able to determine what knowledge it is that's needed at such timely moments. Learning how to acquire knowledge is a matter not only of coming to know how to acquire it but also of coming to know how to acquire it well. The acquisition of knowledge is not just a matter of technique; it's a matter of judgment.

What's at issue here is the difference between doing something and doing it well: between competence and excellence. A piano player should know how to play the notes on the musical score accurately, to articulate them with appropriate phrasing and in proper tempo. These skills are matters of technique. Although they are obviously necessary conditions for being a pianist, they are not sufficient. To be genuinely a pianist, not merely a piano player, a person must also be able to interpret music, to see through the notes to the meaning of a composition, so that the playing brings out the composer's intent and then goes beyond it in order to explore new possibilities the piece might also implicitly contain. Such a person has not only technique but artistry. So also with respect to the acquisition of knowledge. We want young people to be more than competent. We want them to be more like pianists than piano players.

It may strike you as odd to be arguing that librarians should be concerned for the artistry of database searching. However, we all have our tales to tell from the low-tech days of 3 × 5-carded subject catalogs when a student we knew or a faculty colleague–or, yes, ourselves–wasted hours wandering around in a fruitless, because artless, search for subject headings relevant to a proposed project. *Yahoo*, *First Search*, and the Library of Congress on-line catalog increase the content of the subjects available for our possible use by a couple of magnitudes and offer searches not dependent on pre-defined subjects or key words. But students, colleagues, and ourselves can end up just as easily, probably more easily, wasting precious hours looking in the wrong places for the wrong things. High tech tools don't eliminate the need for artistry: they enhance it. But because even an ill-considered search using them might reap a seemingly bountiful harvest, we easily forget the invariant truth for all information searches, high tech or low: garbage in garbage out.

Recall Francis Bacon's metaphor about the difference between ants, bees, and spiders (Bacon, aphorism xcv; however, I've combined the role of the bee and the spider). We don't just gather information like an ant, expecting that after a sufficient amount of it has been accumulated the answer we are seeking will pop up more or less automatically. Like the spider, we must come to the data with a hypothesis already spun, expecting to trap certain answers in our web, and succeeding or not depending on how well made our snare and how well positioned. The ant has an effective technique, and works long and hard using it to find and gather in the resources necessary to fulfill his needs. The spider's artistry is to concoct a strategy by which those resources will come to her rather than her going after them, presenting themselves for her use in timely fashion and adequate supply.

The spider's secret is in part the web she weaves: it should have a mesh fine enough to catch the prey she seeks, coarse enough to let through the insects she has no interest in, flexible enough to bend with the wind and to provide her prey, once caught, no leverage for breaking free. But the spider's secret is also in knowing the place where best to weave her web, the orientation most likely to intercept the purposes of the creatures she finds most to her taste. So also we, in our search for information: the secret lies in knowing what sort of web to weave and where best to weave it. The challenge lies in selecting the most likely place to look and then selecting the tool probably best suited for exploring that sort of place. If these selections are rightly made, the information we seek then comes to us like the fly to the spider's parlor, eagerly offering itself up for our enjoyment.

The problem with selection, of course, is that what we want may be hiding amid what we think is only dross. Or the results of our selectivity may be so plenteous or complicated that, although we have actually acquired what we want, we don't recognize it hidden amid the abundance. Our hypothesis might be falsified, or it might turn out to be unfalsifiable: on the one hand, not compatible with the facts; on the other hand, compatible with any possible fact. For either reason, the web will need to be discarded and a new one strung. But not arbitrarily: for the negative answer always points toward a new selection of what question we should ask or of what to ask it. The old question needs to be narrowed or broadened, pruned or cross-bred, simplified or deepened. Then re-asked, and more likely than not again adjusted and once more asked, and again and again, until a satisfactory answer is finally provided.

The artistry required here is not only skill in selecting where first we should look and by what method, but also the ability to discern what answers are relevant and what ones beside the point. This artistry must then find expression in its determination of whether the relevant answers are confirming or disconfirming, and if the latter how a negative result might serve to improve upon the sort of question asked or the way by which it is asked.

So far removed are these judgments from what a computer, that great wizard of technique, can manage, that the most promising kinds of search engines now being developed are ones that require the crucial intervention of the inquirer's artistry at an early stage of any search. For example, after processing a request for material on a topic which an inquirer thought to have been adequately defined by certain words and phrases, the search engine returns to the inquirer a first batch of candidate answers, typically about twenty, and asks the inquirer to sort them into relevant and irrelevant categories, then to rank the relevant ones from best to least fitting. The search engine, its criteria for generating data now honed by the inquirer's second judgments, then provides results that significantly improve upon what would have been generated on the basis of the inquirer's first judgments only (Allan, J.). And we are all familiar with the cruder but still useful "Refine" option beside the *Alta Vista* "Search" button. Having received thousands of hits too many to our query, we are invited to inspect a parsing of the words involved and to eliminate those we think may have broadened the scope of the information too generously.

[Begin First Parenthetic Aside:] Gentle Reader, please understand this and subsequent asides as the equivalent of long footnotes in the style of 19th century scholarly tomes. They are important contributions to my overall argument, even though they will strike you–because they are–as intrusions into its linearity.

What I'm saying is hardly new news, since librarians at the Reference Desk have been attempting to make more or less this same point for as long as libraries have thought it appropriate to provide their patrons with assistance in finding things. But the glitter of high tech can be blinding and its complexity daunting, so the temptation has often been great for reference librarians to think they should dispense with developing in library users the artistry of information retrieval and be content instead to teach them the techniques for using the new technologies. Any idiot could be expected to find the author area of the card catalog and open the drawer that contains entries on Mark Twain (the "C" drawer, right?), but knowing the techniques for running an *Encore* search for a citation from Shakespeare seems at times as much an accomplishment as learning rocket science.

But even rocket scientists do not easily grasp the peculiarities of proprietary computer terminals and the keystrokes involved in navigating an arcane on-line database. So it is easy enough for librarians to spend all their time explaining how the equipment works and never quite getting to the point where they are able to take it for granted. They find themselves behaving as though they were graduates of those mythical education courses in which teachers are taught how to run slide projectors rather than how to teach.

It sounds obvious when said, but it is not always so obvious in practice: the job of a librarian is to help students learn how to learn for themselves. It's to be a teacher, not a techie. [:End First Parenthetic Aside]

Unfortunately, this distinction between technique and artistry creates an awkward complication for my insistence that the job of librarians is to be good teachers. I've argued that we need to distinguish between techniques for acquiring information and the art of deciding which techniques to use, including when and where and why to abandon them for other ones. Another way to put this distinction is to suggest that besides rules for processing information we also need rules for using such rules. There are rules but there are also rule sorters. Now here's the rub: we can be taught to use rules but we can't be taught to sort rules.

It's easy enough to teach the rules. For every outcome desired there's a procedure for achieving it, a set of instructions which if followed will implement the procedure and so realize the outcome. You want a chocolate cake, you follow the recipe. You want all the scientific journal articles published since 1920 in English or German concerning the Burgess Shale fauna, you set your *First Search* parameters accordingly and press "Start." Rules are algorithms: plug in the initial conditions and they unfailingly churn out the appropriate results.

Granted, the rules we want to teach our students are not those for making cakes or finding articles on Cambrian softbody arthropods. We want our students to learn generic rules: rules for following instructions in cookbooks, rules for doing any article search whatsoever. And granted also, students don't really know the rules if all they can do is repeat them verbatim. They need to be able to use them as well. Were your course on information retrieval to have a final exam, it should take the form of problems requiring fresh thinking and careful judgment. The exam should not ask for a list of the spices used in Betty Crocker's devil's food cakes, but students instead should be given a recipe they've never seen and instructed to follow it, the quality of their work to be evaluated by how close their results come to those of an expert recipe-follower. They should not be asked the date when Whittington published his first article proposing a new taxonomic classification of the *Marrella spendens* organism, but they should be asked instead to find materials on pre-Cambrian organisms that they think would be helpful in understanding the Burgess Shale controversy.

Even given these caveats, however, it is nonetheless true that rules are just exactly the sort of things one teaches, paradigmatically so. They can be identified, articulated, memorized, recalled as needed, put to good use or bad. They can be written on blackboards, posted on webpages, and printed in newspapers. They can even be incised into the granite archways over library entrances as the normative governing conditions for the way the university or the nation should function.

Rules are so easy to teach, indeed, that no human need be involved. It takes real living breathing librarians to formulate information retrieval rules in the first place, but once they have been set down the process of transferring them from the librarian's mind to the mind of a student is just another instance of the mapping process that computers do so well. Self-instructional programs are the way to go when it comes to teaching rules, because the learning process can then be paced to the interest, competence, and convenience of the learner, tailored to that person's unique situation. Most menu-driven computer search engines are simply fancy versions of the old-fashioned self-instructional programs pioneered by agricultural extension services for teaching farmers a specific set of rules by which to increase their acreage yields.

There are no rules for sorting rules, however, no algorithms, for deciding which subject to run your search on and for deciding which search tool to use. And where what needs to be learned isn't a rule, no nonhuman substitute for a human teacher will do. This is only out of the frying pan into the fire, however: for what doesn't fall under some rule or other, what doesn't have a framework of theory sustaining it, can't be taught. And what good are teachers for learning something if it can't be taught? What good are librarians as teachers if deciding how to go about an information search isn't a teachable skill? The answer is that precisely what teachers are for is helping students learn what they can't be taught.

We don't need teachers to teach what can be taught. We need them to create contexts for learning, to provide students with tough-minded critiques and tender-minded encouragements, to play the torpedo fish to their self-satisfied arrogance and the midwife to their creative birth pangs. If teachers, including librarian teachers, do these Socratic things, then their students will learn the artistry of rule sorting I'm arguing they need to learn. Dewey would then be pleased, for we would be understanding the librarian's job as a pursuit of what he told us was the true aim of a student's schooling: learning how to acquire knowledge when it's needed. As teachers who no longer think of themselves as teachers, librarians would have given up trying to do the students' thinking for them. They would be following Rousseau's dictum to let the students do their own thinking as best they can.

So you teach your students some techniques, high tech and low tech, for acquiring information. Then you give them an assignment: learn about a particular subject matter and at an agreed-upon time teach what you know to the other students in the class. You might ask your students to explain the second law of thermodynamics, for instance, or to assess the new Globe Theatre's inaugural performance of *Henry V*, these assignments due for class next Thursday. The students, using tools to which you have introduced them, will then set about acquiring information they think relevant, organizing it as they think appropriate, and devising a way they think effective for communicating what they've learned to the others in the class.

The Internet, should it be one of the resources they utilize, will provide them with a wonderful array of university courses in which the second law is explained, applied, illustrated dynamically, and properly situated within thermodynamic theory. There's even a website containing a loud argument against creationism and another featuring a seemingly irrelevant burglar-meets-parrot joke. In their websearch for *Henry V* the students will need to unravel the confusion of an Old Globe Theatre in San Diego and a New Globe in Toronto before finding the one on London's Southbank. But it will be worth the journey because they'll find there everything from worldwide newspaper reviews of the production to a video of the cast in rehearsal.

What your students will find, of course, is too much, and the fulsome whole of it will come with no *Good Housekeeping* seals of approval by which to distinguish the junk from the gems. So they will make a number of unfortunate decisions regarding what to include, and perhaps by good luck or exquisite insight they will also uncover first-rate material wonderfully apt for their purposes. They will on some occasion take optimal advantage of what they have; on another, they will be dazzled by superficial glitz and bored by dull profundity. And their plans for class may at times seem to you little more than a compendium of all the bad examples from their remembrances of professors past, although they just might surprise you in the end by their ingenuity extempore.

When it's all over, your task is to point out to them the pluses and minuses of their judgments. In your own inimitably gentle, bemused, unpatronizing style, you are to provide a critique of their activity. What were the tools they used needlessly or forgot to use? What sorts of data did they think likely to be worth gathering, that they surely should have had the foresight to know would not be? Conversely, what data that they didn't include should they have anticipated the need for? How did they go about deciding what to keep and with what to dispense, when to narrow their inquiry and when to broaden it, and how might they have been more sure-footed or efficient or effective?

In my example the librarian's critique comes at the end of the whole project rather than at some timely point during the data-gathering phase. I've done this on purpose, because the worth of the data is a function of the end project to which they contribute. Only from the standpoint of the class actually having had to suffer through student amateurs lecturing them opaquely on the second law, or actually having been caught up in a group effort to themselves re-enact the drum-and-staff crescendo leading to Chorus's opening invitation, will you have sufficient grounds for your assessment of the strengths and weaknesses of the information they found. And only from that standpoint at the endpoint will the students have sufficient first-hand experience to appreciate your assessment.

Then it's time for another assignment, time for a new venture among on-line catalogs, websites, databases, government documents, video clips, and all the rest, time for a new struggle with winnowing and extrapolating, focusing and segueing, time for a new effort at pedagogy. Comes the reckoning after this first iteration, and you will find some improvements and some backslidings. Your admonitions will in some cases have taken root and produced a goodly harvest, but in other cases it will be as though you were sowing dragons' teeth. Nevertheless you tell your tale of woe and praise, you point the lessons to be learned, and then it's time for the next assignment in the endless *corso e ricorso* of education.

[Begin Second Parenthetic Aside:] **The usual educational division of labor, confining the librarians to the retrieval of the resources and the course instructor to the pedagogical use of those resources, just won't work**. If what happens is to be genuine learning rather than merely teaching, librarians are going to have to be in the classroom and instructors in the library, working as a team, with students, not just on their behalf.

A technique has its own independent integrity; it's a module that can be inserted where relevant, where opportune or indispensable. But the art of selecting which technique is needed or useful for a particular situation requires an awareness of the whole. If the only role a librarian plays in the learning process is providing an instructional module for students during the first week on how to use the on-line catalog and to find their way around the Reference shelves, then all the librarian can do is teach some data-gathering techniques. It will be up to the course instructor to do the more difficult, and the far more important job: assisting the students in learning how to use those techniques properly.

Librarians as hired guns will never get the respect they crave, because anyone would immediately recognize them for what they are: technicians rather than pedagogues. The valuable Monday morning quarterback is the person who has been privy to the whole experience of the game, whether as player or as spectator, and who seeing it holistically, its details vividly integrated, can then discern why the plays weren't working or why they were. The critique of what the students have done calls for 20-20 vision; only in hindsight can you ever see well enough to be able to make useful, insightful comments. Unless you have the whole to look at you won't have seen enough and so will have no way to see it well. Or, to shift my cliches to a more sophisticated medium, only in the graying dusk can the owl of Minerva begin its flight toward an understanding of what that day's accomplishments have been.

Make the importance of a librarian's full participation clear to your faculty colleagues, protective of a status quo that privileges their place in the educational process. Make it clear to your administrative overlords, fearful of any changes that might require them to run the risks involved in attempting a reconciliation of clashing viewpoints and authorities. Librarians of the world, arise, you have nothing to lose but your status as expendable appendages to the educational enterprise. [:End Second Parenthetic Aside]

Aristotle makes a distinction in the *Nichomachean Ethics* between two kinds of things people do. They attempt to understand the world around them and they attempt to change it. The first sort of activity is theoretical; the second, practical. To do either of these things well, says Aristotle, is to be wise. If you are good at theorizing, your wisdom is theoretical (*sophia*); if you are good in practical matters, your wisdom is practical (*phronesis*) (Aristotle, Book VI; see also Allan, G. Chapter Four). It is this practical wisdom toward which I've been gesturing when I talk about the artistry involved in making good choices. Aristotle's *phronesis* is often translated as "prudence," but it suits our contemporary idiom best, I think, to translate it instead as "good sense."

Aristotle says that theoretical knowledge is teachable because it is governed by universals, by general laws of which particular events are instances. Given knowledge of a law, you can explain, and therefore predict, the behavior of its instances. The fall of an acorn or the growth from it of an oak can be explained by showing that what happens in each case obeys a law of nature: a law concerning bodies in motion and a law concerning the generation of organisms according to their kinds. By reference to the former law, we can predict that an acorn, when detached from its location on a particular oak branch, will seek its natural home, its state of rest, in contact with the earth. Similarly, in accordance with the latter law, we expect that the seed harbored by the acorn will unfold under the influence of its final cause from a potential to an actual oak tree. You and I today subscribe to different natural laws than those Aristotle formulated, but his point remains valid: if the existence and motions of a thing are rule-governed, then a knowledge of that thing can be taught by teaching the rules of which it is an illustration.

There are no rules of good sense, however. In the practical affairs of life, the judgments we need to make are based on our assessment of the particular features of specific situations. The factors involved are uniquely configured; our lives are lived amid historical contingencies. There is no general kind of which these practical situations in which we make our choices are instances, so there is no rule that describes what it is essential we do, that can predict the consequences of acting in one way rather than another. This absence of governing rules is not just the result of inadequate knowledge, although that is often enough the case in such matters. It's rather that the relevant scientific laws abstract from precisely the unique particularities that are often what is practically most important. We need to do something to save this specific person, this child of ours, from drowning; being able to predict the likely rate for accidental deaths during the current year is the farthest thing from our mind. The roll call is about to be taken and we've got to cast our vote for or against the campaign finance reform bill, even though we still have no clear idea of how our constituents and benefactors will react, much less whether the changes it mandates will achieve the ends for which they were designed.

We recognize in others, and in ourselves, the difference between making practical choices wisely and making them foolishly. The ability to exercise these kinds of practical judgments well is a respected and desirable quality. We want those who have demonstrated their practical wisdom as our public leaders, for instance, and we acknowledge, sometimes ruefully, that leaders with good sense exist in a democracy only if the voters have the good sense to elect them to office. So unless you believe that good sense is an inherent quality, something you have to be born with, you will grant that it must be something that can be learned. But political good sense is learned not by sitting in a classroom taking careful notes while a professor lectures on the five necessary steps for becoming a leader. The learning comes through the doing. In practical matters, you learn to make wise choices by making choices and then discovering from that experience how you could have done a better job had you chosen differently or been more sensitive to certain factors, had you given them more of your attention or decided not to be distracted by them as much. You develop a skill for which there is no formula; you acquire an artistry.

Learning good sense in how to go about acquiring knowledge is not something a student does solo, however. As Freud and Sartre remind us, we are never our own best judge (St. Paul and then Augustine were there first, of course, but "sin" is such a turn-off concept these days whereas "repression" and "bad faith" have a *je ne sais quoi* about them that gets even a librarian's attention, right?). Conversation is therefore crucial: face-to-face interactions between yourself and the students wishing to acquire your librarian's good sense. The art of making sensible judgments is always sensitive to context, so a critique of the students' judgments is best made through a concrete exchange between them and yourself. The conversation is not among equals, but it is nonetheless a conversation. You are there to help them develop their artistry, not to substitute yours for theirs. Your role is as someone familiar with the specific context in which they had been making their judgments, perhaps having actually witnessed their choice-making, who is also respected for his or her skill in such matters, a person with good sense.

A conversation is called for, not a sermon or a lecture, nor a check-list of your right answers against which theirs are marked and a grade provided to the registrar or released to the local newspaper. For what is needed are your judgments in dialogue with their judgments, your experienced good sense interacting with their fledgling good sense. You come as the wiser voice to the conversation, but you come only as one of the voices, recognizing that you have no corner on truth, no protection against making a mistake. Your critique is thus part of a mutual exploration of the worth of the students' judgments, an exploration from which you will gain insight as well as providing it, presumably providing more than you gain but never only providing.

Although you can leave all of this to the disciplinary specialists if you wish, your faculty colleagues, you need to be a voice in these conversations precisely because you are not the denizen of some disciplinary specialty. You have your specialties in librarianship, of course, but you were trained to be a generalist with regard to the content of the library's resources and the modes of its access. You are prepared to answer anyone's basic questions about what the library contains and what libraries and other information sources all around the world contain, because if you don't know roughly what's there you won't know how best to find it. Or more to the point, you are confident that you know how to go about finding an answer to questions about what's available where and why and how.

This confidence is not merely your trademark. It's the trademark of the sort of person you want students to be. Librarians are, or should be, exemplars of good sense regarding the identification and retrieval of information. Your role in the education of students is to assist them in becoming like you. Not to become librarians. Heaven forfend! But to become, as good librarians should be: liberally educated voices in the conversation of humankind (Oakeshott; see also Allan, G., Chapter Five). Your expertise has little to do with what students need to learn from you. What they need is your inexpertness, your sense for how best to go about the tasks upon which expertise is dependent. A disciplinary specialist knows a great deal about a specific field of inquiry, but remember that this expert had first to be an amateur who wanted to know more about that field. The amateurs, the neophytes, the apprentices, in a subject area need first to learn how to become more familiar with a body of material in order then to become more familiar with the materials that will soon comprise their expertise.

The learnedness of experts must always be scrupulously distinguished from the knowing how to know that is its precondition. In this sense we are all always amateurs, and librarians are our role models. Or as Socrates famously put it, explaining how he differed from one of the self-proclaimed experts of his day: "it is likely that neither of us knows anything worthwhile, but he thinks he knows something when he does not, whereas when I do not know, neither do I think I know" (Plato, 21d).

Your task isn't to help students find the right parcel of information but to help them know the right way to go about finding it–even if sometimes the right way gets the wrong results. There's a right way for a quarterback to throw a football. It involves teachable techniques: knowing how to grip the pigskin properly, developing strong shoulder muscles and a good wrist snap, and honing one's eye-hand coordination. But the right way to be a quarterback also involves good sense: making judgments about where to throw the ball, how hard, at what moment, and at what acceptable risk. A good quarterback has this know-how, and we can recognize he does even if on any given occasion his judgment may be wrong and the pass knocked down or intercepted. In the long run and for the most part, good football sense pays off in ways that mere technique does not.

Similarly, your students don't learn from you a fail safe decision procedure for acquiring relevant information. Not only will their judgments often prove unwise, for they are apprentices after all, but your critique of their judgments will not always be on the mark. Good sense is not the ability to avoid mistakes but to learn from making them, how to avoid making them unnecessarily. Good sense is always only approximate, the best choice thought available given the relative opacity of the context and the relative unpredictability of the consequences. Good sense is knowing that you do not know, cannot know–and yet must choose.

This is what education should be all about: students learning how to use the tools of learning wisely. The high tech stuff is about the latest tools we have available, and the changing times constantly alter what we want to learn and for what purposes. But new goals and new tools for reaching them still depend on people being able to determine how best to go about deciding which goals are worth pursuing and which tools are worth using in their pursuit. The tough questions still remain how best to understand the goals and the tools selected, so as to use them in a way appropriate to their nature in order to achieve goals for which they are a suitable means. Making effective use of the 21st century library calls for learning new techniques for retrieving information concerning new fields of expertise, but it calls also for learning how to go about sensibly doing these things. And the only way to learn to be sensible is the old fashioned way: by experience critiqued and refashioned constantly in conversation with those more experienced in the search for knowledge.

[Third Parenthetic Aside:] I keep referring to undergraduate students as the patrons you are serving, but everything I've said applies to graduate students and to your faculty colleagues as well. Scholarly research conducted by white-coated scientists in laboratories and tweedy humanists in library carrels is, after all, only a more sophisticated kind of learning than the learning undertaken in classrooms. Your task as a librarian in relation to scholars is more daunting than your task in relation to students. But not because the requisite information is more complex or subtle and the pathway to its acquisition more strewn with pitfalls and false scents. It is more daunting because the greater expertise of your scholarly patrons tempts them to think they do not need you as their critic, their mentor, and–yes, even this–their role model.

The librarian becoming and remaining a voice in the conversation of a sophisticated research program, even that of the most high-powered, grant-laden, and prize-bedecked faculty, is an educational aim every bit as important, every bit as normative, as the librarian being an active voice in the conversations of undergraduate pedagogy. If for no other reason, librarians are needed alongside their faculty colleagues to save them from the consequences of their slow slide into the academic isolation that results from the faculty's current inability to realize that expertise and narrowness are not the same thing, that specialists who are not also generalists soon lose their way because they cannot distinguish what they know from its significance. [:End Third Parenthetic Aside]

Teaching that doesn't teach but that creates dialogical contexts for learning is difficult because not formulaic, not a matter of following the rules, of playing by the book. Acquiring good sense with regard to acquiring information is difficult for the student and for the librarian as mentor and critic. But as Rousseau says, the art of being a good educator is not making things easier for students but making them more difficult. Not making things so difficult that learning becomes impossible, but not making them so easy that it becomes impossible. Rousseau, in good Aristotelian fashion, points the middle way: education is leading students into situations that call for thought, that require the skills of information gathering, imaginative reflection, experimentation. But having led students to a place where perceptive thinking is required, a genuine educator must not then do that thinking for them. The thinking the students need to do will be difficult if the situation is as it should be: one in which the right answer is not obvious, or one in which even the question that needs asking is not obvious, and where at times it will turn out there are no answers nor even any right question. For the librarian or any other teacher, what is difficult at those moments is not being of help. The admonition "don't do something, just stand there" seems backwards and probably un-American, but it is how the teacher best moves the learning process along. The art of learning with difficulty is thus an art the teacher practices by knowing when not to teach, an art the student practices in those contexts where what can be learned can only be learned after the teaching has stopped.

Librarianship appropriate to the information age and the global village, as librarianship when Socrates wandered the Athenian agora or Rousseau was busily prescribing Emile's curriculum, is the art of making it difficult for students so that they can learn to cope wisely with the ardors of the greatest of human tasks: the lifelong search for truth, justice, and happiness. Why the emphasis on difficulty? Because, as Spinoza insisted, "all excellent things are as difficult as they are rare" (Spinoza, 223).

REFERENCES

Allan, George. *Rethinking College Education* (Lawrence: University Press of Kansas, 1997).

Allan, James. "Relevance Feedback With Too Much Data." *Proceedings of SIGIR* (1995), 337-343.

Aristotle. *Nichomachean Ethics,* in *The Basic Works of Aristotle* (New York: Random House, 1941).

Bacon, Francis. "The New Organon," Part II of *The Great Instauration,* in *The Works* (New York: Garrett Press, 1968).

Dewey, John. "Education as Natural Development." *Schools of To-morrow,* in *Essays on Education and Politics 1915 [The Middle Works, 1899-1924, Volume 8]* (Carbondale/Edwardsville: Southern Illinois University Press, 1976-83).

Oakeshott, Michael. "The Voice of Poetry in the Conversation of Mankind," in *Rationalism in Politics* (New York: Basic Books, 1962).

Plato. *Apology,* in *The Collected Dialogues* (Princeton: Princeton University Press, 1963).

Spinoza, Benedict. *Ethics* (London: J.M. Dent & Sons, Ltd., 1989).

From Transmission to Research:
Librarians at the Heart of the Campus

James Wilkinson

SUMMARY. Current changes in higher education practice and think-ing recognize that undergraduate education has suffered because col-leges and universities have not been teaching as well as they might. These changes carry both promise and challenges for librarians. Rising to these challenges is imperative because without the collaboration of librarians, attempts to improve teaching and learning are less likely to succeed. *[Article copies available for a fee from The Haworth Document Deliv-ery Service: 1-800-342-9678. E-mail address: getinfo@haworthpressinc.com <Website: http://www.haworthpressinc.com>]*

KEYWORDS. Undergraduate education, teaching, learning, collabo-ration, pedagogy, Research Model, Transmission Model

College libraries have often been described as the heart of the campus, and for good reason. Their collections nourish scholarship and teaching–which define colleges and universities–while their staffs promote the circulation of materials, without which neither could take place. "Nourishment" and "circulation" evoke the enabling role that libraries have traditionally performed. But they also suggest a broader interdependence: As the heart affects the college, so do other areas of the college body affect the heart.

James Wilkinson (PhD, Harvard University) is Director of the Derek Bok Center for Teaching and Learning, Harvard University, Cambridge, MA 02138.

[Haworth co-indexing entry note]: "From Transmission to Research: Librarians at the Heart of the Campus." Wilkinson, James. Co-published simultaneously in *College & Undergraduate Libraries* (The Haworth Press, Inc.) Vol. 6, No. 2, 2000, pp. 25-40; and: *Future Teaching Roles for Academic Librarians* (ed: Alice Harrison Bahr) The Haworth Press, Inc., 2000, pp. 25-40. Single or multiple copies of this article are available for a fee from The Haworth Document Delivery Service [1-800-342-9678, 9:00 a.m. - 5:00 p.m. (EST). E-mail address: getinfo@haworthpressinc.com].

25

Current changes in the practice of teaching in higher education stem from a recognition that colleges and universities have not been teaching as well as they might and that the quality of undergraduate instruction has suffered. Parents, alumni, and students are asking colleges to become more "learner-centered" and to emphasize inquiry and research at an undergraduate level. Government agencies such as the National Science Foundation, as well as private groups such as the American Association for Higher Education and the Carnegie Endowment for Higher Education, have publicly championed the cause of reform (Hutchings, v).

Changes in pedagogy carry both promise and challenges for librarians. As students are being weaned from traditional lecture courses, the materials available for research are expanding as never before. Information technology enables faculty and students to gain access to a cornucopia of digitized data with unprecedented breadth and depth. And this creates a dilemma. As growing numbers of neophyte researchers confront a growing expanse of information, students' ability to make use of library resources suffers. More people with less training are being asked to do more difficult things–with predictable results.

One solution to this dilemma, I propose, consists in librarians aligning more closely with the teaching community as staff whose skills can serve the educational enterprise in new and broader ways. Current attention to student learning represents a genuine opportunity to redefine relations between librarians and faculty, the reading room and the classroom. **Without the collaboration of librarians, attempts to improve teaching and learning are less likely to succeed.** What might otherwise seem like special pleading on the librarians' own behalf actually strengthens the drive toward making inquiry and investigation key activities of undergraduate education.

As a prelude to concrete suggestions for collaboration between librarians and faculty, it may be useful to outline the principal changes in the teaching and learning paradigm that expand the teaching role of the library. Some are undoubtedly acquainted with these changes and their rationale and may wish to skip the next three sections on changes in teaching practice and move directly to the subtitle "Librarians and Learning." Since the partnership I envision requires understanding both the new pedagogy and the concerns that motivate its defenders, other readers may find a refresher course useful.

FROM TEACHING TO LEARNING:
HISTORICAL BACKGROUND

The reform movement in teaching is not new. John Dewey, among other pioneers, outlined its essential elements nearly a century ago. "It is not the business of the school to transport youth from an environment of activity into one of cramped study of other men's learning," he wrote in 1916, "but to transport them from an environment of relatively chance activities (accidental in the relation they bear to insight and thought) into one of activities selected with reference to guidance of learning" (Democracy and Education, 274). Yet despite Dewey's warning, deference to "other men's learning" has characterized American higher education for most of the intervening years. Knowledge flows from the top down, in this view, passing from teacher to student, from expert to novice. The teacher is accorded the respect due the collective labors of that long line of thinkers and researchers, artists and academicians of whom she is the living representative. The student, for his part, is an apprentice whose largely empty mind awaits the store of knowledge that the teacher will transmit. A perfect match.

One appeal of that traditional view of college teaching was precisely that it assigned clear and unambiguous roles to teachers and students. Inside the classroom, professors lectured; students listened and took notes. Outside the classroom, professors engaged in research and writing; students studied, read, and did their homework (or borrowed it if time ran short). Contact between teachers and students, as befitted relations between unequal partners, remained largely restricted to office hours and occasional questions before or after class. This freed faculty to deliver their insights into *Beowulf* or the Kondratieff cycle with minimum student interference and maximum efficiency. Students, in turn, were expected to reproduce these insights as faithfully as possible. If the student could write an essay at the end of the semester that was virtually indistinguishable from Professor Krump's lecture on the same topic, that feat of mimicry provided strong evidence that learning had occurred.

This state of affairs has come to be known as the Transmission Model of teaching–also sometimes termed the Banking Model, since faculty "deposit" knowledge which students "withdraw." According to the Transmission Model, knowledge resembles an object or sub-

stance, like money, or a book passed from hand to hand, or a liquid poured from one container into another. Think of the lecture hall as a soup kitchen. The professor stands behind a steaming cauldron of knowledge, wielding a large ladle, while the students line up dutifully for their daily rations, bowl in hand. Young minds seeking sustenance drink their fill of academic soup, a hearty broth distilled from scholarship stretching over many years.

The soup analogy, however, fails in one important aspect: While a soup cauldron can be emptied, a professor's lecture notes can be used year after year without change. The professor, that is, does not cease to know his subject once the lecture is over. Nor is the transfer complete. Even the most gifted students will not extract all the intellectual nourishment of lectures devoted to *Beowulf* or the Kondratieff cycle. That awaits graduate study and further training in the field. But to the extent that professors pass along the contents of their lectures (as reconstituted by their students), knowledge does indeed become an object—notebooks filled with writing, to be consulted after class and on the eve of the final exam. I still possess several fat volumes of lecture notes, some thirty years old, as testimony to my skills as an undergraduate scribe. And I suspect I am not alone.

EDUCATING THE PARROT

The Transmission Model remains the dominant teaching mode on a number of campuses, where professors continue to lecture and students continue to take notes as of yore. But this model has also sustained serious critiques from various quarters since Dewey's time, particularly during the past two decades. Most damaging has been the assertion that transmission encourages superficial reproduction rather than genuine learning. There is a cartoon that exemplifies this critique, featuring a parrot whose proud owner is showing a visitor a truly awesome array of framed diplomas on the wall. "Well," says the owner, "he's only a parrot, but as long as he can repeat precisely what he hears, he can continue to get college degrees from any school in the country."

Faculty who correct their own exams recognize that students, unlike this parrot, do not repeat what they hear without error. Their essays resemble instead a game of "telephone," where the sentence whispered in John's ear by Professor Kantor at the start of the chain ("I'm going to Paris this summer") becomes distorted by the end ("I'm growing pears for the plumber"). One reason for this distortion is that not a great deal of thinking occurs while students take their notes. They sit and transcribe. Another reason, paradoxically, is their desire for things to make sense. If what the professor says confuses them, they will invent a plausible alternative. Thus another argument against the Transmission Model is that it promotes errors in replication, since it offers no means of testing these errors against evidence revealed by individual inquiry.

What has most strengthened the hand of the critics, however, is evidence that even students who appear to grasp the material (an impression based on high scores on standard tests) may fail to understand that material on more profound levels. Like the parrot in the cartoon, they look like they know what they're talking about until you start asking them to take what they memorized and apply it to some new situation. Then they fall mute. In one example well known to the physics community, Professor David Hestenes at Arizona State University decided to test the conceptual understanding of students who had taken an elementary mechanics course there. His questions required no computation, but asked students to predict the trajectory of various objects subject to various forces. Those who understood concepts such as force and momentum, he thought, would have no difficulty.

Thirty-six such questions were given to students drawn from four different lecture courses in elementary physics. All but a tiny fraction did poorly on the exam. Asked to make predictions on the basis of conceptual knowledge, rather than to plug a series of numbers into a formula, the students were stumped. They had no idea whether a falling object released at an angle continues to fall at that angle or falls straight down. If a hockey puck traveling in one direction was hit in another, would it go off at an angle, or in a curve? These questions were novel, even if the concepts should have been familiar. As a result, only a few students in the class met the challenge successfully.

The problem with traditional teaching (as this example illustrates) is that it teaches so poorly. When physics students took the same test at the beginning and end of the introductory course, their results showed an average gain in basic knowledge of 14 percent. That is not much. As Hestenes and his co-author noted in a summary article: "Our diagnostic test results show that a student's initial knowledge has a large effect on his performance in physics, but conventional instruction produces comparatively small improvements in his basic knowledge" (Halloun and Hestenes, 1048). In other words, whereas conventional teaching had little effect on these students, their initial preconceptions have a far greater effect on how they understand the material than did classroom instruction. And what little students do learn, they often learn on their own. The idea that students know things that they have largely taught themselves supports the alternative teaching model below.

So what *will* have an effect? To ensure that students actually understand and can apply concepts, something else is needed besides speed writing and memorization. Hestenes and others have argued that we can do better than the Transmission Model. But what would an alternative model look like?

AN ALTERNATIVE MODEL

An alternative teaching model would be designed to follow more closely how learning actually occurs. It would chart the chain of events that leads from (relative) ignorance to (relative) mastery and propose a classroom strategy that includes them all. For example, we could postulate that five steps must occur before students actually understand material well enough to pass Hestenes's concept test: (1) curiosity (the "need to know"); (2) questioning; (3) hypotheses based on the questions; (4) information gathered in response to the hypotheses; and (5) a conclusion (hypothesis confirmed or refuted by the information). Listed in sequence, they are:

1. curiosity (the "need to know")
2. questioning
3. hypotheses based on the questions

---

4. information gathered to test the hypotheses
5. a conclusion (hypothesis confirmed or refuted by the information)

Notice that in this model the transfer of information, that substance being ladled out to students in a traditional lecture, comes relatively late in the sequence as step four. Information is not the first, or even the most important part of learning. It is a tool needed to solve a problem, rather than an end unto itself.

I have taken the liberty of inserting a line between steps three and four. One way to understand the challenge to the Transmission Model is that it focuses attention on the steps above the line, those which precede information. It points to what needs to happen *before* students line up at the cauldron of knowledge, bowls in hand. All too often, lectures provide answers to questions that students have not yet formulated–which have never even occurred to them to ask. The *Treaty of Versailles* in 1919 imposed a heavy reparations burden on defeated Germany. So? Do we really care? But if we ask how it might be possible to prevent Germany from threatening its neighbors in the aftermath of World War One, then heavy reparations are an answer. In the effort to make learning more efficient, faculty skip the crucial issues of awakening curiosity, helping students ask questions, and thinking about plausible answers (hypotheses) first. This is precisely what happens in research. If we were doing research on the reparations issue, we would start with questions, such as the purpose of reparations, or the reasons for their lack of success. That should happen in teaching as well.

Thus a possible and practical antidote to the failure of learning that occurs in the Transmission Model would be: research. Research, that is, undertaken by students with faculty supervision, or, as Dewey put it, "activities selected with reference to guidance of learning." Surely one of the principal fruits of academic study must be an understanding of how to acquire understanding–not just by looking something up in an encyclopedia (though that may be a place to start), but by asking questions, formulating hypotheses, and testing them with data. After all, the factual content of many of the courses taught in the academy will change in the next few decades. In every area of life and work, students will need to solve new problems every day. If faculty persist in handing out only the neat and tidy results of research to students, without ever initiating them into the investigative process that generated those results, how can they learn to investigate on their own?

Enter, then, the Research Model. It offers to make good on many of the failures of Transmission. "Active learning," "student-centered classroom," "problem-based teaching," "case-based learning" are among other common terms applied to the new paradigm. Like members of a large family, these techniques differ somewhat, yet are recognizably akin. All share common assumptions about the importance of students to be doing more than just taking notes. Teaching and learning are seen as more collaborative than unidirectional, more horizontal than vertical, stressing communication between teacher and student, with an open-endedness that comes from a focus on inquiry. They recognize that students must ask questions *before* consuming information. As a result, these alternatives propose a higher standard for learning than what we might call the "parrot test." They expect students not merely to reproduce what they have heard, but to apply it with insight and understanding.

The Research Model is now challenging the Transmission Model on a number of campuses (as well as in pre-college education). With the new model, the definition of "teacher" has broadened to include not just faculty, but students, and, yes, librarians. This is not the same as an egalitarian classroom (or, as some critics suggest, the blind leading the blind). Instead, the metaphor often used is that of a coach or guide–someone who has been over the terrain before, and will help one traverse it without major mishap. But students still have to do the walking. Neither the most accurate and eloquent traveler's report, nor the most technically sophisticated visuals can replace the experience of actually getting up (and down) a mountain on one's own.

Students, interestingly, may at first feel confounded and even cheated by the Research Model. They (or their parents) are paying a great deal of money to be taught. Why do they have to find out things on their own? Especially things the faculty already knows? Why can't Professor Jackson just tell them the answer and cut out the hard work of inventing the wheel? To this plaintive query there exist at least two answers. The first is that students are more likely to understand and remember something that they have figured out by themselves. In the language of developmental psychology, processing information through inquiry increases the chances that this information will move from short-term to long-term memory, and thus be available for recall later (e.g., after the course has ended). The second answer is that we are trying to teach students not simply a body of knowledge, but a method: not simply content, but process as well. We are trying to initiate the students into those crucial first steps of curiosity, questioning, and formulating hypotheses that underlie problem-solving in the real world.

This is especially true of general education or core courses, which have increasingly become an important part of the undergraduate curriculum on many campuses. General education courses can be justified by the intrinsic worth of Shakespeare or Plato, of course. But they are even more justifiable on the grounds that they introduce students to a variety of modes of inquiry and problem-solving approaches. That was certainly the hope of those who crafted the Harvard Core program two decades ago. The description of the program's aim, which echoes that of many other forays into general education, reads in part:

> The Core differs from other programs of general education. It does not define intellectual breadth as the mastery of a set of Great Books, or the digestion of a specific quantum of information, or the surveying of current knowledge in certain fields. Rather, the Core seeks to introduce students to the major *approaches to knowledge* [italics in original] in areas that the faculty considers indispensable to undergraduate education. It aims to show what kinds of knowledge and what forms of inquiry exist in these areas, how different means of analysis are acquired, how they are used, and what their value is. (Courses of Instruction, 1)

How does one study a "form of inquiry"? By asking the sort of questions and applying the sorts of tools appropriate to a broad field of research–moral philosophy, or art history, or physics. General education, in other words, makes the Research Model even more germane.

LIBRARIANS AND LEARNING

This long prologue has outlined the changing pedagogical landscape into which we are all entering. In one sense, librarians enter especially well equipped. After all, librarians know something about research. As its importance grows in the undergraduate curriculum, so does theirs. And if more teaching and learning now take place outside the classroom, with an emphasis on research or research-like activities, then this opens yet another path for librarians to join the teaching/learning enterprise. Further, given the flexible format of much of the new teaching, collaborative efforts are now encouraged to a greater degree than ever before.

An example is a recent query that went out among a group of faculty from several institutions about expanding their class materials. These faculty explored, via the Internet, the possibility of giving students specific and timely information concerning international affairs, and then using this information as the basis for class discussion. They traded their favorite IR issues and attendant documents back and forth, and helped one another assemble a stock (one might say a "virtual library") of teaching materials for common use. Here is an example of the intersection between the availability of data and new possibilities for student learning, as well as of the strengths of collaboration. Once faculty seldom revealed their teaching practices to one another; now, as we will shortly see, they need the help and support afforded by collegiality in the classroom.

For as the definition of teacher has broadened, so has the definition of sources on which student learning is based. Traditional sources-books, journals, archives, audio tapes, photographs, slides, posters, and the like-remain important. But they have become supplemented (though not supplanted) by a wealth of new additions, ranging from source books compiled thanks to Kinko's photocopiers to CD-ROMs, courseware, and, of course, the Internet. Thus the shift toward the Research Model coincides with a burgeoning field of new products on which that research can be practiced. Libraries continue to function as repositories, like the great library of Alexandria. But they contain greater riches, and communicate more readily with other libraries, both real and virtual, than ever before.

The use of objects in the library-be they traditional or electronic-should be to stimulate learning. And here we encounter a paradox. For just as the holdings of libraries have increased, so the ease with which they can be brought to bear on research has simultaneously diminished. The faculty discussing new materials for teaching international affairs on-line huddled together, electronically speaking, in order to help find useful data. None presumably had the time to slog through the total mass of information available on even a single current hot spot such as Bosnia. A researcher (faculty *or* student) who looks up a keyword such as "Bosnia," or "inflation" or "Milton" cannot possibly even check the relevancy of the titles, let alone read the literature revealed by the search (Wilkinson, 185-86). Welcome to the world of information overload.

Discussions of information technology (IT) and the new directions taken by teaching often suffer from two misconceptions. One is that IT and the new pedagogy are somehow in harmony, simply because they are occurring at the same time. In fact, with a few notable exceptions, early attempts to integrate IT into classroom practice have shown their lack of harmony far more often than their synergy. Put bluntly, most software is too stupid to allow for the unexpected, and the unexpected is precisely what the Research Model attempts to foster. Thus we have the paradoxical situation of the latest technology serving outdated teaching aims, and the latest teaching being unable to use much of IT.

Technology threatens either to make students too passive, or to inundate them with too much information. Their passivity results from programs that provide video "enrichment" with no need to think or solve problems. A CD-ROM entitled "From Alice to Ocean," for example, allows one to follow a trek from the Australian outback to the shores of the Indian Ocean, but prevents students from asking their own questions or doing much more than clicking the mouse at appropriate intervals. Not much research there. But the information glut constitutes a still more serious issue. Nowhere, to my knowledge, have those who design databanks seriously debated the disadvantages of having too much information. Like money, more is presumed to be better. And we are all, it seems, eager to accumulate as much as possible. The U.S. Census Bureau offers us the latest census data on-line; NASA's web site allows us to download the latest views of space as recorded by the Hubbell Telescope. Journal articles, vote totals from the Indian parliamentary elections, and continuous global weather data crowd the Internet. Information stretches as far as the eye can see.

How do we survive the rising tide of information? Though it may seem counterintuitive, one important role that librarians can serve in the new teaching paradigm is to protect both faculty and students from data overload. Librarians can help direct students and faculty to the most promising sources; they can also help them hone their digital skills on the Internet. The burgeoning variety of resources makes guidance all the more important, especially since, as noted at the start of this article, most students, at least, have very little training (if any) in the research game.

Genuine research starts with a question or questions, as we have seen. Equally important, however, is the ability to distinguish between more and less promising questions. Some may be too broad, some too narrow; some trivial, others requiring a lifetime of study. Like Goldilocks, students may have to sit in various chairs and try eating soup from various spoons before they find one that is "just right." In the Transmission Model, students fill in the outlines, like preschoolers with a coloring book. In the Research Model, they take more initiative. The hierarchical concept of knowledge passing from the top down is replaced with a more democratic concept of collaborative inquiry. A salient aspect of this initiative lies in devising fruitful lines of exploration, and knowing how to pursue them as a team.

Of course, one characteristic of research is precisely that its early stages make it difficult to distinguish between more and less fruitful questions and more or less useful information. While one is refining one's question, and making preliminary forays into the archival underbrush, it is easy to go astray. But going astray may also prove productive. Not all "mistakes" turn out to be a waste of time. A student who tries to dig up information concerning Thomas Jefferson's Louisiana Purchase may find that the topic is too broad, but that the Aaron Burr conspiracy involving General James Wilkinson, which he stumbled across in the course of looking into the former topic, is just the thing. Research (like life) is messy and unpredictable. Librarians can at least help distinguish between wasted effort and productive mess. For example, they can reassure students that much apparent waste is in fact normal and productive, and remind them that skills in the research process may matter more in the long run than the narrow research outcome of this particular effort.

George Allan argues this issue in "The Art of Learning with Difficulty" that "to know how to go about learning things is far more important for students than what they've learned." I wholeheartedly agree. Of course, inquiry cannot be taught in a vacuum. That is to say, course content provides a necessary vehicle for learning "how to go about learning things." A course that simply investigated the theory of learning would do little for most undergraduates, since what they need is practice doing inquiry in a particular discipline. Furthermore, that practice (Allan's "how") will vary from field to field. The mode of inquiry in history overlaps with–but is not identical to–the mode of inquiry in medicine, or English literature, or urban sociology. The research model assumes that content is not an end in itself, but a means to a greater end, which is learning how to learn.

THE LIBRARY CHALLENGE

Triage, even within the more challenging parameters of the information revolution, still belongs within the traditional purview of the reference librarian. The greater challenge for librarians is to go beyond even the complex role of guide to the information superhighway, and to enter the new world of Research Model pedagogy as partners with faculty.

Librarians, of course, have always taught. Whenever they explained the holdings of the library, or the methods best suited to retrieving *New York Times* articles on microfiche, or how to get the reel-to-reel audio tape to work, they assumed a teaching role. But this role has most often been related to step four in our model, the step that relates to conveying information. Librarians have known where information resides in the heart of the campus. The Research Model, on the other hand, gives questions a new prominence as the engines that drive inquiry. Thus librarians may wish to become involved earlier in the learning process, back at the first step, where students' curiosity is whetted, or at the second step, where questions are being formulated. In addition to giving guidance about information itself, they can also help students and faculty consider which questions are most appropriate, given the resources available for research in different domains.

Starting at the point where learning involves asking questions suggests two specific challenges for librarians. First, they can help faculty understand the teaching potential of the library *within* the new paradigm. They can explore what projects it makes possible and how they could be integrated into existing courses, what archival collections are available, and how could they be used most imaginatively for undergraduate projects. I imagine a series of coffee conferences, with faculty invited from related disciplines such as American history and American literature, where such questions would be posed. "We have a complete collection of yearbooks from Warren Easton Boys' High School in New Orleans starting from 1927–how might they be used for an investigative project in modern American social or education history?" Faculty could be drawn to explain their educational goals for a specific course, and librarians could then think *with* them about how specific library resources might support student work in pursuit of those goals.

The second challenge involves helping students to frame questions, rather than just find information. Perhaps librarians might do this in tandem with faculty, perhaps on their own. I imagine a taxonomy of questions posted somewhere near the card catalogue (or on-line), divided broadly by field, with grand but unwieldy questions ("Why did the Civil War begin?") contrasted with narrower but more useful ones ("Why did the state of Georgia vote to secede from the Union?"), and some hints on how to gauge which is which. Students need coaching in the art of asking good questions–questions, that is, that lead to learning. They need to see how a question might play out in terms of time and research effort. And here librarians, knowing the available resources as they do, can offer especially valuable assistance.

But they should not offer *too* much. George Allan calls this paradoxical skill "not being of help." Not helping constitutes the exact antithesis of the Transmission Model. For instead of handing information to the student, a space of tension is created within which the student is encouraged to investigate something on her own. That something needs to answer a question that students care about (see steps one and two above), via a process of discovery that teaches the student that she *can* discover things on her own. Teachers are proud of what they know; librarians, in my experience, are proud of knowing the tools required for inquiry. That constitutes a certain advantage over faculty. Faculty may be tempted to give answers to students in their field of expertise. Librarians, on the other hand, will be less tempted, since their area of expertise is the research process itself. They are hence less likely to rob the student of the sense of accomplishment that comes from successful (and minimally aided) discovery.

A good example of how learning can be facilitated without spoon-feeding the student is a technique elaborated by Prassede Calabi (with funding from the National Science Foundation) to sharpen learners' questioning skills. Teachers and students of ecology were asked to observe a nearby habitat (a park or a vacant lot near the school), sit alone for a half hour, and write down twenty-one questions. There was nothing magic about the number twenty-one, but the more questions the better. Anything that struck learners as interesting or odd deserved inclusion in the list. "Where did these plants come from?" "Why are there crickets, but no butterflies?" "Does noise from nearby traffic affect animal life?" And so forth. From each person's list of questions, participants then selected their top or "burning" question, which they shared with the (reconstituted) group. The group discussed each question in turn, making suggestions about how it might be expanded or focused. In the end, the group decided which questions to pursue, and which experiments might lead to answers (Calabi, 493).

The sense of how best to help the beginning researcher–or even the more advanced faculty investigator–comes with practice. Where possible, I would suggest that librarians begin that practice on themselves.

A version of Calabi's "21 Questions to Conclusions" can be applied, for example, to the pedagogical challenges facing library staff. At the teaching center that I direct, librarians come together on occasion to pose questions relating to their craft, such as "How do you help students at the start of their first year?" or "How do you handle disruptive questions?" or "How does one calibrate information to audience members at different levels?" We have then circulated the questions within the group, and then met again to discuss those that seemed especially "burning." This exercise has the advantage of modeling what may be an unfamiliar teaching technique on safe ground, and with the promise of outcomes of direct benefit to the participating librarians.

Perhaps the moment has come to put in a good word for teaching centers. As the director of one, I am naturally biased in their favor. Yet I also know how teaching centers can help to link libraries and librarians with the classroom. At Harvard we regularly and successfully invite librarians to participate in our training programs for young faculty and graduate teaching assistants. If anyone on your campus knows about both the promises and the pitfalls of the Research Model (or active learning, or whatever its local label), then it is likely to include folks at the teaching center–should you be lucky enough to have one. They can suggest readings, lend videotapes of exemplary teaching, even observe sessions where librarians attempt to expand their teaching skills and offer feedback. A library-teaching center alliance promises important benefits for both groups.

The Research Model makes possible and delivers, improved student attitudes and better student learning. But implementing it is not easy. It demands different skills and more overall effort from the teacher. The fact that students assume a more active role in the classroom makes the teacher's role more complex–a point often forgotten in discussions of the new pedagogy. A key component of that complexity is getting students motivated. Whereas teachers once exercised "control" directly (through lecture and the syllabus), now teachers act more indirectly, through questions, group facilitation, and as guides. Only indirectly can they inspire student motivation, without which neither research nor class discussion will succeed. This means knowing students in new and perhaps unfamiliar ways. Thus even faculty who wish to adopt the Research Model may experience a steep learning curve, lasting several semesters. They need whatever help they can get–including the help of librarians.

Because the Research Model requires that we understand the links between curiosity, questioning, research, and information in a deep and integral manner, it worries me that some advocates of active learning adopt its procedures piecemeal. They do not seem to grasp that the model works only as an integrated whole. So, for example, it does little good to prompt students to ask questions if there is no thought given to follow-up projects, or to invite discussion and then pre-empt it with a mini-lecture. As the questions from the Harvard librarians illustrate, group dynamics alone can play a major role in the success or failure of a more open-ended, participatory style of teaching.

In order to spread and invigorate use of the Research Model, we need to be concerned about raising the level of teaching skills among faculty and among librarians. If it is to be fully successful, the Research Model must be more than a set of slogans or gimmicks. It has to transform fluid moments into learning opportunities. The strength of the Research Model, after all, is its potential to help each student think and understand. That is also the strength of the library and its staff. There, at the heart of academe, the synergism between these two strengths should grow and nourish the academic enterprise in ways we can only begin to imagine.

REFERENCES

Calabi, Prassede, "Technique: 21 Questions to Conclusions," in *Ecology, A Systems Approach: Teacher's Guide* (Dubuque, Iowa, Kendall Hunt, 1998) 491-98.

Dewey, John, *Democracy and Education: An Introduction to the Philosophy of Education* (New York: Free Press, 1944).

Halloun, Ibrahim Abou, and David Hestenes, "The Initial Knowledge State of College Physics Students," *American Journal of Physics*, vol. 53, no. 11, November 1985, 1043-55.

Harvard University, *Courses of Instruction, Faculty of Arts & Sciences, 1998-99* (Cambridge, MA, 1998).

Hutchings, Pat, *Using Cases to Improve College Teaching: A Guide to Reflective Practice* (Washington, DC: American Association of Higher Education, 1993).

Plato, *Works, III: Lysis, Symposium, Gorgias,* trans. W.R.M. Lamb (Cambridge, MA: Harvard University Press, Loeb Classical Library Edition, 1925, reprint 1996).

Wilkinson, James, "Homesteading on the Electronic Frontier: Technology, Libraries, and Learning," in Lawrence Dowler, ed., *Gateways to Knowledge* (Cambridge, MA: MIT Press, 1997).

Librarian as Teacher:
A Personal View

Howard L. Simmons

SUMMARY. Though I discovered what it meant to "learn how to learn" as a lifelong student almost fifty years ago, my learning curve about the librarian's role has evolved and grown progressively more sophisticated. My personal contacts with school librarians and later as Executive Director of the Middle States Commission on Higher Education with library deans convinces me now more than ever that the most effective librarians in the new millennium will be those who empower learners and who facilitate the teaching and learning process. *[Article copies available for a fee from The Haworth Document Delivery Service: 1-800-342-9678. E-mail address: getinfo@haworthpressinc.com <Website: http://www.haworthpressinc.com>]*

KEYWORDS. Librarians as teachers, lifelong learning, information literacy, teaching, learning, mentors and mentoring, bibliographic instruction, accreditation

Though I discovered what it meant to "learn how to learn" as a lifelong student almost fifty years ago, my learning curve about the librarian's role has evolved and grown progressively more sophisticated. As has been the case with my overall cognitive development and the consequent acquisition of knowledge and skills in other areas,

---

Howard L. Simmons (PhD, Design and Management of Postsecondary Education, Florida State University) is Professor, Educational Leadership and Policy Studies, Arizona State University, Tempe, AZ 85287-1006.

[Haworth co-indexing entry note]: "Librarian as Teacher: A Personal View." Simmons, Howard L. Co-published simultaneously in *College & Undergraduate Libraries* (The Haworth Press, Inc.) Vol. 6, No. 2, 2000, pp. 41-44; and: *Future Teaching Roles for Academic Librarians* (ed: Alice Harrison Bahr) The Haworth Press, Inc., 2000, pp. 41-44. Single or multiple copies of this article are available for a fee from The Haworth Document Delivery Service [1-800-342-9678, 9:00 a.m. - 5:00 p.m. (EST). E-mail address: getinfo@haworthpressinc.com].

my knowledge of libraries and of the role of librarians in them has gone through stages. From the earliest to the present stage, I have been fortunate to have the benefit of influential persons in the library field beginning with the late Mrs. Edith McClain, my high school librarian and teacher/mentor. What I learned from her in the 1950s shaped forever my perspective of the librarian as teacher-mentor and learning facilitator. It is within this context that I share my views about the real role of the college and university librarian.

My first real learning facilitator, Mrs. McClain, was, by anyone's standards in the segregated South, a properly credentialed school librarian. Broadly educated in the liberal arts, she had a Bachelor of Library Science–the professional credential at that time. More than that, she had a strong commitment to helping students "learn how to learn." She decided to make me her unofficial student library assistant and that experience served as a beacon for my interest in libraries and my early faith in librarians as mentors, teachers, and facilitators of learning.

Though school authorities made limited resources available to "colored schools," Mrs. McClain was a genius at making the wise selections. I watched and listened intensely as she explained to other students how to find information (long before information literacy programs were in vogue), as well as how to evaluate that information for specific use. Against the odds and under the most wretched conditions that could befall an academic library, she was a quintessential information specialist and my role model as a teacher and end-user of information resources. While I never forgot the important, secondary roles of librarians as custodians, guardians and curators of books and serials, I have continued to appreciate those roles within the context of a more important one: the teaching role of the librarian.

When I matriculated to college, I found another librarian-mentor in the person of the late Ms. Marie Jaubert. Ms. Jaubert, the Spring Hill College librarian, allowed me to serve in the payless role of "student library assistant" and to play the role of learning facilitator by helping other students and patrons become more information literate. Until assuming that role, I didn't appreciate fully how much I had learned about library research from Mrs. McClain and from a former high school English teacher, Mrs. Naweta Brown Pinkney. Because of the teaching influence of Mrs. McClain, Mrs. Naweta Brown Pinkney, and Ms. Jaubert, I had "learned how to learn."

As a faculty member and administrator, my beliefs about librarians as mentors, teachers, and learning facilitators continued to grow. It wasn't until I joined the professional staff of the Middle States Commission on Higher Education, however, that I became an advocate for libraries and librarians. When promoted to Executive Director of the Middle States higher education accrediting commission, I pushed colleges and universities to adopt stronger bibliographic instruction and information literacy programs for students, working to add to the *Characteristics of Excellence* (the Middle States' statement on standards for accreditation) a comment on the essential need for an active and ongoing bibliographic instruction program. When I met Dr. Patricia Senn Breivik, the Dean and Director of Libraries at Wayne State University and the Founding Chair of the National Forum on Information Literacy, my learning curve came full circle. Dr. Breivik's work in information literacy and resource-based learning confirmed my long held conviction that most librarians are, first and foremost, teachers.

Now more than ever, I am convinced that the librarian in the new millennium will be pushed even more in this direction by a variety of forces both within and outside of the library profession. External forces include advances in technology and the advent of the information age. Internal forces include an evolutionary process of re-definition in light of those external forces. It is heartening to note that the profession itself in a recent ALA "Report of the Steering Committee on the Congress for Professional Education" (ALA, June 1999) recognized the need to examine "traditional roles, new roles, additional roles, enduring roles" and to "Position Librarianship as the 21st Century Profession" (Internet: http://www.ala.org). Although the report itself clearly demonstrates some ambivalence among librarians about joining forces with other information specialists, the profession's commitment to change is expressed in the original focus of the Congress, which was "to examine the initial preparation of professional librarians as a first step in studying the broader issues or education and training for librarians and other library workers."

The challenge for the profession will be the continuing education of thousands of librarians who are already in positions that can have enormous influence in the current efforts of the profession to re-define or extend itself into other information domains. As one library school Dean (Swigger, 1997) states the following in an abbreviated paper found on the Internet:

Continuing education will be necessary not only because technology and practice change, but also because librarians move through different stages of responsibility and opportunity in their careers. A major challenge for library education–which may or may not be the responsibility of university library schools–is to provide the continuing education that is so vital. Librarians' knowledge needs evolve as their careers mature, and as working conditions change. Right now, there is a serious need for a formal structure for continuing education, perhaps including certification of some kind at various stages. In the next century, meeting the need for continuing education will be as important as meeting the need for education for new librarians.

No matter what librarians are called in the profession or how much more technology is used to access information through the medium of library and information resources, the most effective librarians in the new millennium will be those who empower learners and who facilitate the teaching and learning process. Since my learning quotient about libraries and the role of librarians began almost fifty years ago, **I am convinced that the re-definition of the librarian's role as teacher-learning facilitator–and not technology per se–will be the most constant factor in the empowerment of learners and their outcomes.**

REFERENCES

American Library Association, *Report of the Steering Committee on the Congress for Professional Education*, June 1999. Internet: http://www.ala.org

Swigger, Keith, "Education for an Ancient Profession in the Twenty-first Century" (Adapted from a Speech Presented at the Military Librarians Workshop, November 20, 1996). Internet: http://www.ala.org

Creating Learning Libraries
in Support of Seamless Learning Cultures

Steven J. Bell

SUMMARY. Higher education has been rethinking the traditional teaching paradigm of the lecture in which most faculty-student interaction occurs in the classroom. The new emphasis on student learning focuses institutional mission on enabling learning by whatever means work best. Creating a seamless learning culture is one way to stress student learning. A significant feature of seamless learning is supporting out-of-the classroom learning. This paper examines how academic libraries can contribute to a seamless learning culture and what this means for restructuring approaches to library instruction and the ways librarians interact with students. *[Article copies available for a fee from The Haworth Document Delivery Service: 1-800-342-9678. E-mail address: getinfo@haworthpressinc.com <Website: http://www.haworthpressinc.com>]*

KEYWORDS. Learning libraries, learning communities, seamless learning, bibliographic instruction

THE SCENARIO

It is 9:00 a.m. on a Thursday morning at a typical college library. This undergraduate campus is in the midst of the spring semester. Students are inundated with exams and papers. An influential humani-

Steven J. Bell (EdD, University of Pennsylvania; MLS, Drexel University) is Library Director at Philadelphia University, Philadelphia, PA 19144 (address e-mail to: bells@philau.edu).

[Haworth co-indexing entry note]: "Creating Learning Libraries in Support of Seamless Learning Cultures." Bell, Steven J. Co-published simultaneously in *College & Undergraduate Libraries* (The Haworth Press, Inc.) Vol. 6, No. 2, 2000, pp. 45-58; and: *Future Teaching Roles for Academic Librarians* (ed: Alice Harrison Bahr) The Haworth Press, Inc., 2000, pp. 45-58. Single or multiple copies of this article are available for a fee from The Haworth Document Delivery Service [1-800-342-9678, 9:00 a.m. - 5:00 p.m. (EST). E-mail address: getinfo@haworthpressinc.com].

ties professor and her teaching assistant walk in through the front entrance. They proceed to the reference area, shouting loudly: "It is 9:00 o'clock in the morning and there are no students here. What are the librarians doing?" Librarians within distance come forward, puzzled.

The professor explains that her assistant is a residential advisor. He has observed students in the dorms at late evening hours, when they really start studying and writing, at a complete loss for using library resources. The professor says, "When our students really need help from you folks, you're not here. No one needs you at 9:00 a.m. when you're staffed as though you expect an onslaught of students. We need you when the students are ready to learn, and where the learning takes place. What are you going to do about it?"

The professor makes a good point. Most college library reference areas are void of patrons in the morning hours, yet library administrators continue to maintain a reference desk presence to handle requests for assistance that are few and far between. Where are the patrons? Asleep or in class. More likely, the decline in visits to the reference desk, not just in the morning but throughout the day, signals a more ominous phenomenon: significantly diminished building traffic. The culprits are generally perceived to be the Internet and the library's ability to migrate what were in-house resources to the Web. With virtually every database now deployed on the campus network and distributed to desktops on and off campus, fewer patrons need to visit the library to perform research. Has the profession laid the groundwork for its own obsolescence? No.

An argument could be made that academic libraries are in the vanguard of a new and dynamic rethinking of higher education in which the focus is shifting from teaching to learning. A variant of this movement is known as seamless learning. Put simply, seamless learning creates a campus culture that recognizes that students also learn out of the classroom. It provides a structure for an organization to fully capitalize on how and where students learn best. Having created academic libraries "without walls," the profession is far from obsolete. It is instead well positioned to blend into the new educational culture. The challenges are how to best accomplish the transition from teaching library to learning library and how to respond to faculty, like the professor in the scenario above, who demand that librarians give more attention to students whenever and wherever they need help.

TEACHING AND LEARNING:
IS IT MORE THAN JUST SEMANTICS?

A landmark article in the November/December, 1995, issue of *Change* began a movement to rethink fundamental premises. Barr and Tagg, authors of "From Teaching to Learning–A New Paradigm for Undergraduate Education," suggested that the new paradigm for education should focus on learning, not teaching (Barr and Tagg, 13). In the learning paradigm the institutional mission enables learning by whatever means works best. This shift in thinking was a reaction to the traditional teaching environment for undergraduate students: the passive lecture-discussion where professors talk and students listen. The new learning paradigm recognized that there is a place for the lecture-discussion, but that it alone fails as an optimal setting for student learning.

Calls to change the traditional undergraduate education model were more than reactions to the weaknesses of teaching-centered education. They were also motivated by economics. Employers wanted knowledge workers, employees able to use information to obtain new skills and apply what is learned in productive ways. The traditional teaching paradigm focused on short-term memorization of facts and didn't prepare students to continually discover, synthesize, and apply classroom material to solving emerging problems. Traditional teaching was failing to produce the type of worker that industry wanted. Creating those individuals, educational institutions were realizing, was not the sole responsibility of the teacher and would occur only when education extended to all campus venues.

A changing sense of mission among college and university administrators also contributed to the shift in emphasis from teaching to learning. Many administrators and faculty now define learning more broadly and believe that colleges and universities must do more than teach students a set of courses in preparation for a career or advancement to professional school. The college experience should help qualify students to assume citizenship responsibilities.

Noticing that many students were politically indifferent, unfamiliar and apathetic about other cultures, and generally lacking the readiness and the intellectual curiosity to succeed in a 21st century multicultural and global environment, institutions began extending learning beyond the confines of the classroom. To develop better prepared students, they developed new programs that required faculty and student life professionals to link what students do in the classroom with their out-of-class activities. Good examples include the many "First-Year" programs adopted at academic institutions. Beginning in the freshman year with readings and events that define a theme for the college experience, freshmen are exposed to a broad range of programming that contributes to a holistic learning environment.

THE NEW LANGUAGE OF LEARNING

The new educational paradigm has added new educational terms: seamless learning, learning colleges, learning communities, learning organizations, distance learning, and self-directed learning. What distinguishes these concepts and programs from one another? How do they differ from seamless learning, which stresses the importance of out-of-class learning and may afford library professionals the best opportunity for active involvement in the educational process?

Similarities

The new learning-oriented programs share some common characteristics. First, they recognize the need to rethink traditional teaching methods. Second, they suggest that this rethinking and experiments in restructuring the campus educational system should center around the needs of the learner. Third, they recognize the importance of situational or experiential learning as a supplement to lecture-style teaching and the value of collaborative opportunities for students to learn from each other. Comparing three of these well known learning-revolution programs in an article titled, "Learning Communities, Learning Organizations and Learning Colleges," Terry O'Banion (CEO and President of the League for Innovation in the Community College) identified another commonality: reform efforts were sparked by the 1983 report, *A Nation at Risk,* which sounded alarms over the mediocrity of American students. This report and subsequent ones called for putting student learning first (O'Banion, 1).

Learning Communities

Experimented with for the last seventy years, learning communities are designed to enhance collaboration among students and to create more coherent curriculum choices. Today, the use of learning communities is increasingly popular and widespread. By restructuring the curriculum, the institution creates more intellectual interaction between students and faculty (O'Banion, 2). Communities can even take on different formats, such as the curricular learning community, the classroom learning community and residential learning communities (Wiemer, 7). Within distance learning programs, on-line learning communities are being used to engage remote learners in collaboration with one another.

Learning Organizations

Other colleges and universities are attempting to become learning-centered by re-inventing themselves as learning organizations. The goal is to create a community of commitment among its members so that the organization can achieve its goals. The members of the learning organization continually expand their capacity to learn and to provide opportunities to learn together. Typically, learning organizations develop flattened hierarchies to create worker teams. A learning organization is designed for the staff of the institution, while a learning-centered institution is designed for the students. While the learning organization approach may not be a direct path to enhanced student learning, the processes of these organizations are somewhat compatible with those of a learning-centered institution (O'Banion, 3).

Learning College

A newer approach, the learning college, is closer in philosophy to a seamless learning culture (SLC), though it is typically specific to a community college. The learning college, like the SLC, differs from the learning community and learning organization in that it is a more holistic design. However, learning colleges can both incorporate learning communities and be based on a learning organization. O'Banion describes the learning college as one in which the commitment to placing learning first is of a much more comprehensive nature. Educational experiences for learners can occur any way, any place and anytime. Creating a learning community is a much greater challenge because the institution must move away from the traditional structural and bureaucratic confines that have defined educational institutions for the last one hundred years.

Seamless Learning Cultures

To better understand the SLC, think of all higher education institutions as existing on a spectrum of operative behaviors. At one end are the "functional silos." That is the phrase Ted Marchese, President of the American Association of Higher Education, used to describe institutions in which faculty and staff are isolated one from another by specialization and expertise-driven behavior. Both faculty and staff interact with students, but there is no coordination between the two. At the other end exists a collaborative environment in which faculty and staff work together for holistic student development. The main responsibility for faculty and staff in this environment is to create the conditions that foster learning, while students take an active role in assuming a significant share of the responsibility for their own learning.

Think about the undergraduate's or the graduate student's college experience. What is most memorable about it? When asked, most persons will describe a professor or student life staff member who took a personal interest in their intellectual or personal growth. Most people do not find the institution, their major, or specific classes particularly memorable. For almost all, the most rewarding experience revolved around personal attention, usually received outside of the classroom. That near-universal experience accurately reflects the two most important influences on student learning and personal development: (a) interacting in educationally purposeful ways with an institution's "agents of socialization" (e.g., faculty, staff and peers), and (b) directing a high degree of effort to academic tasks (Kuh, 135).

Every institution wants to improve student learning. The answer for Kuh, a leading proponent of SLCs, is not reducing class size, hiring more highly credentialed professors, sending faculty to workshops where they learn to teach better, or spending more money on facilities. The key is to create conditions that motivate and inspire students to devote more time and energy to purposeful activities, both inside and outside the classroom.

Those conditions exist in an SLC. More specifically they exist in an environment in which students are encouraged to take advantage of learning resources both inside and outside the classroom. In an SLC, faculty and staff use effective instructional practices. Students are asked to use their life experiences to make meaning of material introduced in class and labs and to apply what they learn in class to their lives outside the classroom (Kuh, 136).

Kuh offers six principles for creating an SLC.

- **Generate enthusiasm for institutional renewal:** all members of the institution must work together to link programs and activities across the academic and out-of-class dimensions of students' lives. One or more champions must emerge to take on this challenge and create the momentum needed for change.
- **Create a Common Vision of Learning:** the campus must create a unified vision of how seamless learning will work. "Common" means the vision comes before personal interests. It can begin with a campus-wide discussion of those conditions under which students learn best.
- **Develop a Common Language:** principles of learning organizations can be valuable, but such jargon tends to be off-putting. A common language must be developed to create and communicate what is to be accomplished by the shared vision. SLCs are cultivated when an institution adopts the language and philosophy of talent development to endorse a holistic view of student learning.
- **Foster Collaboration and Cross-Functional Dialogue:** a shared vision of seamless learning is contingent on maintaining open dialogue at the institution. Student affairs professionals must form partnerships with faculty and academic administrators to create the conditions that motivate and inspire students to take advantage of institutional resources for learning.
- **Examine the Influence of Student Cultures on Student Learning:** student and faculty goals clash; students want good grades, friends and a job, while faculty want students to work harder. To get students to change their goals it is critical to understand the social contexts under which they learn. If this culture is not properly addressed, any seamless learning effort will fail. Faculty, through assignments and interaction with students, can begin to develop a culture where their peers endorse hard working students.
- **Focus on Systemic Change:** faculty and student affairs professionals must focus on what students need to learn and create the conditions that will make it occur. "We-they" thinking must be eliminated. A shift is needed from hierarchical administrative behavior to institutional cultures that value partnerships and cross-

functional collaboration. Reward systems should be changed to favor collaboration over independent performance.

Together, these six principles can help institutions achieve an important outcome: deeper learning. The traditional American educational system is oriented to surface learning–memorizing facts for short recall, addressing new topics before previous ones are internalized, and providing limited opportunities for sustained interaction and collaboration.

SLCs: WORTH THE EFFORT

The primary advantage of deeper learning is that it makes knowledge transformational. With it, students develop an understanding of subject matter that allows them to be able to learn about it independently. Deeper learning heightens the intrinsic motivations and natural curiosities that challenge individuals to learn new information or apply knowledge in new ways. The SLC environment facilitates deeper learning by extending the education process beyond the classroom. Faculty and staff work together to create situations that allow students to use knowledge transmitted in the classroom and to do so when they are ready to use it to accomplish something concrete.

SLCs take advantage of the benefits of "situational learning" in which knowledge is situated in practice. For thousands of years people learned new skills as apprentices. Apprentices learned by doing, they always understood why they were learning something, and their learning was "scaffolded" so that each new skill was built on skills mastered already. Education, during the last 100 years, gravitated away from situational learning to the transmission of facts and abstract theory in classrooms. The SLC is a return, in part, to the idea of learning in those situations where students internalize classroom knowledge.

Creating an SLC requires considerable effort. It involves representatives from every part of the institution. Ithaca College (NY) is one campus working to create an SLC. It is a culture where staff members, no matter what job they perform, are involved in each student's education. Campus security workshops on crime prevention offer students the skills they need to prevent them from becoming crime victims on and off campus. Dining services staff have considerable contact with students and use it to help students learn about proper nutrition and eating habits. Most importantly, student life staff work together with faculty to get these staff members involved in the learning process. According to Kuh, the key is to engage students in a variety of learning activities through an institutional ethos that promotes educationally purposeful activities in settings beyond the classroom (Kuh, 11).

LEARNING LIBRARIES AND WHAT THEY DO

Largely because of their delivery of bibliographic instruction programs, many librarians consider themselves teachers. Typically, instructional programs range from one-hour library overviews to semester-long library research courses. They create awareness about library resources. But do they enable students to achieve deeper learning about information competencies? Looking at the numbers of graduates who lack true information literacy, the profession could indeed conclude that while students may learn to use a few specific databases, they are hardly well prepared for lifelong or self-directed information resource learning. **As higher education institutions re-think teaching altogether, perhaps it is now time for academic librarians to restructure their organizations as learning libraries.**

A learning library can be a critical contributor to an SLC, but for this to happen librarians need to look at their facilities as labs for situational learning. Every interaction with a student, whether at a reference desk, an instruction session, or a casual meeting among the stacks can enable a student's learning process. Library skills are internalized through deep learning. That can and should happen in and out of the library. Situated learning occurs when knowledge is gained through practice. In a learning library, bibliographic instructors create practical situations to encourage students to understand why they are learning the research process and how to learn more on their own. The changing nature of resources and how they are used means moving instruction beyond the walls of the library. If the students are not coming to the library, librarians need to go out to them.

The challenge is to move away from traditional teacher-oriented approaches to library instruction that promotes surface learning only and toward methods adapted for the new learning environment. Recognizing that students are more likely to internalize research skills when properly situated is one way to do this. That situation is rarely a regularly scheduled library bibliographic instruction session, but more likely a dorm room at 1:00 a.m. That is the time when a research paper is due in the next day or two and many students are remotely connected to the library's databases. How might a library administrator reorganize a reference department or develop a new service initiative to respond to the professor who pointed out the library's failure to reach students when and where they need librarian assistance?

Library instruction programs alone are unlikely to achieve deeper learning about library resources and information retrieval skills. No series of instructional programs will accomplish that. The across-the-curriculum model that integrates information literacy skills and outcomes, as described in the next paper by Kimberley Donnelly, is a far better approach. When connected with a seamless learning environment, where what happens in the classroom is intertwined with what is happening outside the classroom, librarians may begin to see students who internalize information retrieval skills. Librarians will have evidence that students are achieving deeper learning of library and information retrieval skills when they can go to another college or university library–and with minimal or no assistance–identify the types of resources available, decide which from among them are appropriate to the subject being researched, conduct an effective and accurate search, and retrieve the necessary full-text articles. When students can do that instead of being satisfied with the first two or three pieces of information they retrieve from a *Yahoo* search, then libraries will be learning libraries.

FROM TEACHING LIBRARIES TO LEARNING LIBRARIES: EXAMPLES FROM THE FIELD

Libraries that contribute to a campus SLC have at least one thing in common. They offer programs and services designed to reach students when and where they are situated for learning. That means the students are involved in some type of intellectual or experiential activity where the opportunity to learn a skill is optimal. From the perspective of the librarian, one such opportunity arises when students conduct research for a project. Whether that research occurs in or out of the library, whether it involves print or electronic resources, and whether it is for a highly focused topic or a comprehensive but broad research paper, interaction with a library staff member at the time assistance is needed can powerfully effect deeper learning. What are libraries doing to both create and make the most of these opportunities as they move from a teaching to a learning model?

To date, most efforts have focused on reaching the remote user. Typically, this is the student using the library from a residence hall, but it might be a student living off campus either at home or a local apartment. At one large, research university, the University of Pennsylvania, an innovative program called the 21st Century Wheel Project has created a learning library opportunity. The Project is composed of special residence halls where faculty reside and that attract students interested in the similar subjects or issues. Database logs at the University showed heavy use of library databases from 11 p.m. on into the wee hours of the morning, the exact times when no librarians are available to provide assistance. Realizing that a variety of support needs were going unmet, several departments, Information Technology, Mathematics, Writing, Languages and the library worked together with faculty and student life representatives, to form a "wheel of assistance."

The goal was to provide front line assistance on nights and weekends in the learning houses, as they are called. This was accomplished by hiring students, usually upper-class students, to serve as peer assistants. For the library, one professional librarian coordinates the program, hires the students and trains them, and reviews all peer-student interactions. The program does not simply train students and then let them loose to provide assistance. The assistants are closely monitored, receive on-going training, and also work at the library reference desk a few hours a week. Should an information request exceed the assistant's ability to provide an answer, each assistant is trained to put the requester in contact with a professional librarian. Student assistants are also responsible for publicizing their services. They put up posters in their residence halls, organize database training sessions in the dorms, and encourage students to attend library programs. The program is still fairly new, and there are as yet no evaluations to indicate how it has improved students' information competency skills. But the program is considered a success so far because assistance and support is going to students who would otherwise not be reached.

Although the Penn program does not cost tremendous amounts of money, other institutions may not have even the minimal resources necessary to allow the library staff to offer a service that fits into an SLC. Two other programs, where fewer resources are needed or where resources can be shared, are exploring alternate methods to reach remote users when and where assistance is needed.

The reference department at Temple University, in Philadelphia, is experimenting with technology that will allow reference desk staff to provide real-time interactive assistance to library patrons. The target population for this service is students working in their dorm rooms or in computer labs who need assistance during database search activity and who are currently on-line and unable to use a phone line. A reference desk librarian is alerted to questions–from which database to use to advise how to find information in specific databases–by a beeper at one of the desk workstations. This allows the librarian and requester to chat on the workstation monitor. The library began this service using a low-cost software package called *TalkBack,* but has since developed its own improved version called *TalkNow.*[1] In a short period, the use of *TalkBack* has already outpaced the number of E-mail reference questions received at the library.

Recognizing the vacuum in good reference service to their many remote library users, the fourteen libraries in the Pennsylvania State System of Higher Education joined together to create the Virtual Information Desk (VID). Maintained by Mansfield University in Mansfield, Pennsylvania, the VID is an experimental centralized, digital reference service that can be reached by e-mail and that exists to answer questions from students at any of the fourteen libraries in the system. The desk is staffed primarily at night when students are most likely to be doing library research from their residences. Similar to the program at the University of Pennsylvania, this one uses trained student assistants to answer the questions, and they are supervised by a professional librarian. While the program's design provides service in the evening, usually until midnight, a significant number of questions are received throughout the day, and there is talk of expanding the hours of operation for the VID.

Though none of these institutions has a clearly defined mandate to create an SLC on its campus, the library staff at each has recognized the need for students to receive assistance out of the classroom. Each has begun to expand library learning beyond the traditional confines of the in-the-library bibliographic instruction session. While some of the programs, such as the one at the University of Pennsylvania, are closer in design to seamless learning activities–primarily because they result from collaboration with faculty and student life staff–all the services discussed here move the library in the direction of the learning library. Other libraries need to re-think what happens within their facilities to create a learning environment for students that goes beyond the surface learning that occurs in traditional instruction programs and to position themselves to respond to the fictional professor's, "What are you going to do?" question about serving the needs of students when librarians are either unavailable or students are unable to come to the library for assistance.

CONCLUSION

Is this all just semantics? If students become proficient at using library resources does it really matter whether the Library Director describes his or her organization as a teaching or learning library? Those are merely labels. Ultimately, what counts is creating a vision of and adherence to a philosophy that guides actions. In a true SLC librarians can find a place for both surface and deep learning. Which end of the spectrum is selected depends on the answer to the question, "What do we want students to learn about library research?" Sometimes all that students need to know is what button to click. At other times, the effort to create a situational learning experience for understanding the conceptual foundations of research skills is needed to help students become capable of self-directed and lifelong knowledge acquisition and processing ability.

Perhaps the answer to the question of how librarians should describe their instructional programming is to shift the focus from a single descriptive label to a learning environment adept at providing a range of skills along a spectrum bounded by surface and deep learning. For lack of a better term call it a learning library, which is really not a physical entity at all but a process for educating students about research skills. This process enables students to learn how to think about and use information resources proficiently. They may learn this from a professional librarian, a student assistant, or in team efforts with faculty, and they may learn it in the library training room or the lounge of a dormitory.

As a part of an institutional SLC the library creates an environment that encourages and supports all forms of opportunities for learning. This is how librarians can best help institutions build learning cultures that graduate students who are prepared for the challenges of the new millennium.

NOTE

1. More details about *TalkBack* and *TalkNow* appear in an article authored by Sam Stormont and Marc Meola (Temple University) in the *Reference Librarian* (Fall, 1999).

REFERENCES

Barr, Robert B. and John Tagg. "From Teaching to Learning: A New Paradigm for Undergraduate Education." *Change* (November/December 1995): 13-25.

Kuh, George. "Guiding Principles for Creating Seamless Learning Environments for Undergraduates."*Journal of College Student Development.* (March/April 1996): 135-148.

Kuh, George. "Some Things We Should Forget." *About Campus.* (September-October 1996): 10-13.

O'Banion, Terry. "Learning Communities, Learning Organizations, And Learning Colleges." *Innovation: The Crossroads of Innovation and Creativity.* (April 1999). [Online] Retrieved June 3, 1999. URL: http://www.innovating.com/page_19.html

Weimer, Maryellen. "The Powerful Potential of Learning Communities." (book review) *The Teaching Professor* (June/July 1999): 7.

Building the Learning Library:
Where Do We Start?

Kimberley M. Donnelly

SUMMARY. Educational change and reform are tools for academic librarians to begin building learning libraries. Before beginning construction, however, librarians need answers to two practical questions: What does an ideal learning-centered approach to information literacy entail? Are model programs in place? Searching for those answers will prepare librarians to ride the wave of change from the periphery of the college experience into the heart of students' learning activities. *[Article copies available for a fee from The Haworth Document Delivery Service: 1-800-342-9678. E-mail address: getinfo@haworthpressinc.com <Website: http://www.haworth pressinc.com>]*

KEYWORDS. Learning, information literacy, educational change, college students, learning libraries, requirements

Educational change and reform, as described by many authors in this work, provide the opening into the curriculum that academic librarians need to begin building learning libraries. Higher education institutions embracing the new learning-centered educational paradigm and Research Model of education, that Wilkinson explained

Kimberley M. Donnelly (MSLS, Clarion University of PA) is Assistant Professor and Reference Librarian at York College of Pennsylvania, York, PA 17405-7199 where she teaches "Information Literacy 101."

Address correspondence to: Kimberley M. Donnelly, L105 Schmidt Library, York College of Pennsylvania (address e-mail to: kmdonnel@ycp.edu).

Excerpts of this article were originally published in the December 1998 issue of *American Libraries*.

[Haworth co-indexing entry note]: "Building the Learning Library: Where Do We Start?" Donnelly, Kimberley M. Co-published simultaneously in *College & Undergraduate Libraries* (The Haworth Press, Inc.) Vol. 6, No. 2, 2000, pp. 59-75; and: *Future Teaching Roles for Academic Librarians* (ed: Alice Harrison Bahr) The Haworth Press, Inc., 2000, pp. 59-75. Single or multiple copies of this article are available for a fee from The Haworth Document Delivery Service [1-800-342-9678, 9:00 a.m. - 5:00 p.m. (EST). E-mail address: getinfo@haworthpressinc.com].

earlier in this work, are ripe for innovative information literacy initiatives. Convincing arguments have been made that librarians should be partners or collaborators with teaching faculty in the process of fostering student learning, but to be part of this change librarians need answers to two very practical questions: What does an ideal learning-centered approach to information literacy entail? Are any model programs already in place?

THE LEARNING-CENTERED APPROACH: ANALYSIS AND DESCRIPTION

A learning-centered approach to information literacy is organized formally based on clear information literacy competency standards. In this organized structure, campus experts assume new roles and the campus community exhibits long-term commitment to information literacy through multiple opportunities for application, visibility throughout the curriculum, a collection of core resources, and value-added information systems. In fact, the initiative cannot meet its goals and objectives unless all these are in place. Several libraries have attempted information literacy initiatives, often including pieces of the learning-centered approach, but what makes the learning-centered approach different is its dedication to deep learning among students.

Organization

A formal, concrete, sequenced program forms the core of the learning-centered approach to information literacy. Most current campus information literacy or bibliographic instruction initiatives are hit or miss. By luck of the draw, some students participate in multiple library instructional sessions because they take courses from professors who value research skills and who make time for in-class instruction by librarians. Other students fail to receive any instruction because they select professors who do not schedule the time. In the learning-centered approach, a formally structured program guarantees that all students engage all the important concepts and processes of information searching within the context of their disciplines. While the methods may vary for each major, all students achieve competency. Indeed methods may differ widely from one institution to another, as long as students are regularly (every semester or at least every year) and productively (creating documents, presentations, posters, plans) working with the information search process.

Organizing such a program is difficult. It requires wholehearted support from administration, faculty, and librarians. High costs are unavoidable, and administrative and political problems may stonewall efforts. In order for the program to be successful, faculty members have to be willing to open up class time for teaching information literacy concepts and processes and be prepared to share the classroom, perhaps even entire courses, with teaching librarians. The learning-centered approach requires a new level of information competency of all faculty members.

Likewise, librarians face challenges. Some are unprepared, uncomfortable, or even unwilling to teach (Saia 1995, 4). As they take on new levels of teaching responsibility, they need support and encouragement from experienced teachers. Classroom management, lesson planning, and grading may be new experiences for some librarians. In spite of the various personal and professional issues, a learning-centered approach depends on a mutually agreeable, comprehensive design based on a commitment from the entire campus community. Fortunately, the climate of educational change and reform encourages new roles and attitudes for both faculty members and librarians.

Standards

As with the organizational design for the information literacy program, standards and competencies are fine-tuned at the local level. They provide the content and substance for the learning-centered program. Because information literacy is a hybrid mix of library literacy, computer literacy, technology literacy, and more, each campus community determines an appropriate curricular balance.[1] After defining and approving local competencies, the campus community can select and design requirements encouraging creativity, learning, and transferability. Planning for reinforcement, application and complexity is crucial if the program is to engender long-term learning, comprehension and knowledge. In the second half of this paper, some model programs are described; however, many of these have implemented only parts of a comprehensive learning-centered model. These examples are included to demonstrate possible components of a learning-centered information literacy requirement.

Expertise

Campus communities have the necessary expertise: the learning-centered approach to information literacy programs simply changes the ways that they use that expertise. Campuses have expert teachers on their faculties, so librarians need not recreate that expertise. Similarly, librarians are already the campus experts on the information search process, and computer support staff are already experts on the campus network, software, and hardware. Efficiency and effectiveness are lost when teaching faculty members are required to become information and computer experts (although they must maintain competency) and vice versa.

The issue of expertise unveils problems with the ways librarians and computer support staff have been working. Traditionally, much of these two groups' time has been spent on point-of-use advising–applying expertise only when students have problems or ask questions. In the learning-centered approach, the formal structure integrates this expertise into instruction and assignments. Rather than waiting until students have difficulty using a database or the Web and ask for help, the learning-centered approach anticipates that students will need to make information-related decisions as part of an assignment and supplies the expertise before the student is frustrated or running late.

Naturally, concerns arise about how much of a teaching role is appropriate for librarians and computer support staff. The answer to this question depends primarily on campus climate and philosophy and is determined by the design of the formal requirement. Some campuses want a credit-bearing course taught by librarians as the first stage of the program. Others choose workbooks, learning communities, Web tutorials or course-integrated instruction as the first level. As librarians migrate from the reference desk reactive approach to information searching to a formally structured, proactive involvement in student information-seeking, their roles shift. Whether librarians take the role of teacher, facilitator, collaborator or some mix of the three really does not matter as long as they become involved with students during the steps of the Research Model of education that Wilkinson describes.

Long-Term Commitment

In an essay in the book, *Finding Common Ground*, Gretchen McCord Hoffmann says information literacy has been envisioned, "as a set of definable, obtainable skills, and the process of attaining information literacy as a fixed path to a distinct endpoint. However, the level of instruction that is needed to reach this point requires a great deal of time, and thus is an unrealistic goal for many library instruction programs" (1998, 144). Even if librarians no longer focus on an endpoint, but rather view information literacy as setting the stage for lifelong learning, students need continual, time-intensive contact.

The creation of unified competencies throughout the curriculum is the factor that ensures students are information literate at graduation. The formal structure of the information literacy requirement stretches across the student's college career and continues to build upon the key concepts of information seeking, retrieval, and use. Not only do librarians (and computer support staff) need to be involved at every level of the college experience, but they also need to be involved at every stage of the Research Model of education. By integrating information search concepts, skills, and processes throughout the curriculum, students can learn to transfer these abilities to varied challenges.

Students need to know that efficient, effective information-seeking ability is valuable. Through an institution's long-term commitment to supporting a comprehensive information literacy program, students become aware of the critical role information plays in both their lives and careers.

Application

Learning involves practice. In the learning-centered approach to information literacy, practice is built into the program in tandem with more complicated information-seeking tasks. Students need the experience of applying basic research concepts in more complex ways, as well as exposure to more complex search strategies. As students are asked to apply information literacy skills, concepts, and processes, it is likely that librarians and teaching faculty will need to shift roles. For example, librarians may teach introductory information literacy courses for freshmen, collaborate with teaching faculty to integrate advanced techniques into selected sophomore and junior level courses, and serve as research team members or consultants for senior/graduate students working on capstone projects.

Learning activities encouraging application include requiring students to justify sources in a paper's bibliography or asking them to prepare and include a search plan and notes on their search process as part of an assignment. These types of activities suggest a role for librarians in team-teaching and grading of student information-seeking assignments.

Visibility

When wedded to the mission and goals of the college, departments, majors and library, the learning-centered approach to information literacy is visible to all campus constituencies. Just as institutions demonstrate commitment to writing and critical thinking through across-the-curriculum or intensive programs, so should they emphasize information literacy. As part of a commitment to a campus wide information literacy program, all members of the community must be aware of the program and of its interplay among courses, majors, and departments.

McKenzie (1998, 252) puts this into perspective: "If librarians have the boldness to grasp this . . . option, we might be able to create a new consensus about research in the academy." Any program lacking visibility cannot hope to maintain coherence and consistency for students. Any program not tied to campus mission and goals is easily recognized as fluff by the entire campus constituency.

Common Core of Resources

In order for a campus- and curriculum-wide information literacy program to work efficiently, everyone must be speaking the same language. A campus information literacy web site, textbook or resource collection that is available to all players is crucial for consistency and cohesion. Access to this common core of resources ensures that faculty will be able to facilitate the cumulative building of competency and the transference of skills from one problem to another. At York College of Pennsylvania, a team of library faculty created a prototype of an on-line textbook, called the *IFL 101 eText*, for their two-credit, core-curriculum course, Information Literacy 101 (http://www.ycp.edu/library/ifl/etext/ethome.html). The University of Washington's UWired program provides a core resource, *Catalyst*, for teaching faculty (http://depts.washington.edu/catalyst/home.html). Grassian and Clark list other examples of core information literacy resources in their article, "Information Literacy Sites."

Value Added Information Systems

As Allan notes in this work, today's students confront an "avalanche of information." If libraries and librarians are to focus on student learning and to value students' time, they must provide well-designed library systems, information gateways, local web site collections and other value-added resources particular to the campus.

Sharing expertise in such visible ways proves to students the librarians' commitment to their learning experience. In arguing for a shift to this role, LaGuardia strongly criticizes current practice: "As the information age has advanced over the past 20 years, we have been busily staffing desks at the expense of *devising* new tools for organizing and accessing information" (1995, 9). Although it is important to help students negotiate current information systems, it is even more important to learn when students are encountering technological roadblocks and to work toward creating better systems.

GETTING THE BALL ROLLING: LEARNING-CENTERED APPROACH IN ACTION

For 21st century librarians, the task is to begin shaping learning-centered information literacy initiatives. The key to implementing these lies in nurturing understanding and support from the whole campus community. Doing this requires librarians to demonstrate and document the need for formal information literacy requirements as part of the college's complete program of study and to advocate new initiatives incorporating all the features described above. Top level administrators and faculty recognize the potential of an information literacy program when they are made aware of the knowledge base needed for efficient information-seeking and the teachable nature of information literacy skills, concepts and processes.

Although the body of literature about information literacy initiatives grows steadily, most of it is written by librarians for librarians. The next step is to share information literacy successes, theories, and plans with the broader community in education periodicals and at educators' conferences. In order to garner support, material about information literacy initiatives has to be delivered to administrators and faculty through channels they commonly use. This kind of communication may be the key to establishing respect and understanding throughout the campus community.

Further, proponents of information literacy requirements should base their arguments both on the college's and departments' mission and goals and on accreditation standards. By focusing on the practices and requirements in these documents that the curriculum does not formally support, librarians can design information literacy requirements that fill holes and that become integral parts of students' experience. For example, the proposal for an expanded information literacy program at Florida International University incorporated accreditation criteria from the Southern Association of Colleges and Schools (http://www.fiu.edu/~library/ili/iliprop.html).

THE REQUIREMENTS: A BALANCED MIX OF METHODS

Any number of activities or experiences can fit into the learning-centered approach to information literacy as long as they are appropriate to the campus climate, economy and philosophy; however, the key is the integration of these teachable elements into all areas of the curriculum, including the general education program, area distribution courses, and majors. Because the learning-centered approach to information literacy involves phases throughout students' college careers, librarians have to switch hats as students become more mature information seekers and require different kinds of assistance. In addition, the activities that invite students to practice and prove mastery must change. As a result, a hybrid mix of educational methods and assignments is likely to provide students the opportunities they need.

Some of the methods currently in use by model information literacy programs are described below. These models are included because they demonstrate that information literacy initiatives can be learning-centered. In some cases, the elements described are pieces of larger programs in place on those campuses. In others, the requirement described is a first step toward a comprehensive program. Through e-mail interviews, the author gathered first-hand reports about how these information literacy programs work for students. The intent in describing certain components is to highlight methods that could be combined into ideal learning-centered programs.

Freshman Level

New students need to interact with the learning library early on and the interaction has to be positive, empowering and useful. At the freshman level, students need to be introduced to the basic research processes, concepts and skills in a manner that is relevant to them and avoids insults to their current level of mastery. Many schools are already providing some type of freshman research experience.

Required Courses

Some campus communities select the required, core-curriculum course model as a vehicle for engaging students in introductory information-seeking activities. Generally, these survey level courses are taught by faculty librarians and meet in the library building. A separate course is valuable because it demonstrates the campus commitment to information literacy by making it a course requirement equal to other core competencies like mathematics, writing, speaking, and critical thinking. By placing librarians in a teaching role, these courses can change the way students perceive the library and give librarians more equal footing with other faculty.

Two basic approaches to required courses exist. One is to offer a single course with multiple sections. Naturally, the course setup varies. At York College of Pennsylvania, students take a two-credit, semester-length course. Susan Campbell, Course Coordinator and Library Director, commented, "The very best thing is that it is an integral course in the core curriculum with tremendous support from the faculty, administration, and Board of Trustees. The twenty-six hours of instruction time enables us to impart essential skills and concepts to our students in an exciting, challenging, changing time."

At Marylhurst University, all students participate in "Information Power, CLL 373," a ten-week, three-credit course. When asked why the program works for students, Pierina Parise, an "Information Power" instructor, answered, "We encourage students to take our class in the same term for which they have a research paper to do for another class. In this way, they choose the subject focus of their research, and our class becomes, in effect, course integrated without our having to teach many separate, subject-related classes."

Students at Manhattanville College are required to take "Information Literacy: Critical Skills for a Changing World, LIS 1001," a one-credit course taken in conjunction with the required college writing course. In describing how students react to the course, Susan Rubin, Reference & Instructional Services Librarian, said, "Our course is an essential component of modern education. Many students are initially reluctant to take it; however, by the end of the course, they have a better understanding of the need to know these information gathering and evaluation skills. Often, students come back the next term to tell us how valuable the course has been."

A second approach is to designate individual sections of the course for specific disciplines or majors. At Plattsburgh State University of New York, students must take a one-credit, nine-week course, called "Introduction to Library Research, LIB 101," which is offered in six topic areas: allied health, business, education, nursing, science/math, and arts/social sciences. According to Carla List, course spokesperson, "The variety of sections *per se* is the biggest advantage to offering LIB101 this way. Students have a criterion other than time of day when selecting a section . . . and students see that the course addresses their individual needs" (1995, 394). The course has been a general education requirement since 1979, and is the first step of the school's information literacy program. By creating discipline-specific sections, instructors are able to draw more heavily upon the research tools of a particular field and to create learning groups with shared academic interests; however, the model assumes that students have selected a major and will remain in that field. While many students are motivated by the subject approach, students who change majors during the course may feel that the more targeted course is no longer interesting or worthwhile.

Learning Communities

To assist students in becoming acclimated to a new campus, some schools have implemented learning communities or freshman interest groups (FIGs). Although size and duration of these groups vary widely, they exist to provide new students with a sense of belonging in a vast new system. At Indiana University-Purdue University Indianapolis (IUPUI), information literacy objectives were made a part of the core curricular requirements for the already established learning communities (Orme 1998).

In this way, the basic information-seeking skills, concepts and processes are integrated into every student's course schedule. The learning community model stresses delivering learning opportunities to students outside of a traditional classroom structure, although it may also make use of library orientations, tours, and workshops. At the University of Washington, "A FIG is a group of 20 to 25 new UW freshmen with similar interests enrolled in the same cluster of classes during their first quarter on campus" (http://depts.washington.edu/nsp/fig/fig.html). One part of the FIG requirement at UW is a one-credit seminar, "University Resources, Information and Technology:

GS 199." FIGs are just one part of a comprehensive information literacy program at UW.

Workbooks or On-Line Tutorials

Used separately or paired, workbooks and on-line tutorials can be used to engage students with basic information seeking concepts. Because these tools are well suited to self-paced, self-initiated work, they often appeal to students. These methods shift the workload from teaching to tutorial design and production. The Teaching Methods Committee of ACRL's Instruction Section provides a list of good examples of instruction on the Web (http://www.bk.psu.edu/academic/library/istm/tutorials.html). The Committee on Library User Education at the University of New Orleans has defined a plan involving tiers of information literacy experiences. The second tier of their program utilizes a *Library Skills Workbook* in conjunction with the freshman composition course to familiarize all students with basic information seeking skills (Committee 1998, 131). They anticipate future iterations of the workbook in electronic format.

Course-Integrated Modules for the General Education Curriculum

Freshman students may be targeted for information literacy instruction through the General Education Curriculum. Collaboratively designed modules based upon a formal structure of information literacy goals and objectives can be written into selected course syllabi. Like the learning communities model, the course-integrated model allows for greater individuality of information literacy experiences and emphasizes the fact that research is content driven. At California State University at San Marcos (CSUSM), all general education courses must include an information literacy component. The goal of information literacy is stated on the program's Web site, "The MISSION of the Information Literacy Program is to infuse throughout the curriculum the teaching of information theory, concepts, skills and use of the library to the CSUSM community and formal CSUSM outreach programs, focusing on those skills necessary for accessing, retrieving, evaluating and using information" (http://ww2.csusm.edu/library/ILP/).

One of the biggest questions in developing any course or program is whether librarians should teach research processes without focusing on the content of information. The course-integrated model solves this problem by providing instruction in the context of regular courses. Gabriela

Sonntag, Coordinator of the Information Literacy Program (ILP), explained the CSUSM viewpoint. "The real strength of our program is the fact that it integrates IL instruction into the curriculum. Like Writing Across the Curriculum, we feel that IL cannot be separated and taught on a stand-alone basis. It must be seen as an integral part of the students' understanding of the content." Some of the best examples of course integrated assignments are posted on their course assessment Web page (http://ww2.csusm.edu/library/ILP/course%20descr.htm).

Sophomore and Junior Levels

Traditionally, upper-level instruction has existed for the sake of expediency. It has been more efficient to visit the nursing class in which students are being assigned to use *CINAHL*, rather than to walk sixty students individually through the database at the reference desk. Looking at upper-level instruction through the lens of an information literacy requirement thoroughly changes the purpose and goals of this instruction. Because all sophomores have worked with basic research concepts and processes as freshmen and because specific goals and objectives for advanced information-seeking behavior are written into specific upper-level courses, library instruction is no longer a reaction to an assignment, but the driving force behind its construction. The goals and outcomes for upper-level courses can include tasks specifically intended to reinforce basic information literacy concepts and move toward advanced techniques.

At the sophomore and junior levels, information literacy requirements can ensure that all students are introduced to the literature of their fields. Students may identify prominent researchers for a topic, read professional and scholarly publications, or study primary sources from periods of major change within their fields. Rather than writing traditional research papers, students can be invited to apply the basic and advanced research techniques to creating the kinds of documents and presentations they will be asked to make in the real world, including research articles, review articles, feature stories, editorials, and proposals.

As a word of caution, students do not need to mutate into mini-librarians at any stage of the information literacy requirement. Rather, these upper levels of the requirement encourage students to become educated information consumers. The requirement is successful if students can ask productive questions and identify needs for information, schedule project timetables with sufficient time to unearth or create needed information, and make informed decisions about the information seeking process.

Information literacy requirements for sophomores and juniors may involve integrated modules, which are a part of the syllabus and course goals, or separate advanced information literacy courses, which target the literature of the discipline. No matter which model is selected for upper-level requirements, assignments designed collaboratively by faculty, librarians, and computer support staff provide the opportunities students need to apply and practice information-seeking techniques.

At this level, the tasks assigned to students should marry research process to resource content and guide students into advanced levels of evaluation and source selection as they begin to grasp the finer points of their chosen discipline. Faculty members must be knowledgeable about current research tools in their disciplines and trends in the research and must assume some of the workload of teaching information literacy at this level. At the University of New Orleans, specialized upper-level instruction forms the third tier in their program. Subject librarians are responsible for ensuring that the goals and objectives defined for upper-classmen and graduate students are integrated into the curricula for each department (Committee 1998, 132).

Senior and Graduate Levels

Students who have progressed through the information literacy program to this level should be knowledgeable about information and capable of making information-related decisions. As new professionals, they need access to the level of information-seeking expertise librarians possess. At this stage, librarians are likely to be needed as expert consultants or mentors to student research teams. These students need to work closely with librarians to negotiate complex searching. Advanced information literacy courses may be offered in conjunction with senior and graduate research courses. Students conducting original research may find valuable a seminar focusing on the literature review portion of their projects. Alternatively, advanced skills and outcomes may be integrated into the syllabi for the senior project courses.

Learning-centered librarian intervention for seniors and graduate students should be seamless and individualized, supporting students as they make intelligent information-seeking decisions. In the past, students have been unable to reach this level of information competence because campus communities have not provided the supporting structure that students need. Some schools have offered remedial library skills courses to students doing original research; however, these courses are the equivalent of the freshman programs described previously. Empowering students to become information-seekers making their own decisions requires implementing the entire learning-centered approach to information literacy.

EDUCATIONAL CHANGE AND REFORM WITHIN INFORMATION LITERACY PROGRAMS

As other writers in this publication have stressed, formal information literacy requirements need to be grounded in the "learning paradigm" and to focus on process.[2] Regardless of the competencies identified, the methods selected, and the structure developed, a learning-centered information literacy program has student learning at its heart and infuses information literacy into the entire curriculum in ways meaningful to students in the long term. Students may learn about local resources and systems as a positive side effect of the requirement, but the emphasis is on helping students learn to make informed information-seeking decisions.

Carla List says, "The concept-based approach is significant. Most of us (librarian-instructors) try hard to get the students to focus on the process of research rather than on which button to push when. This means that we try to get them to make decisions consciously, based on an understanding of the way the information is stored and how it's retrieved." If the initiative is to be valuable to students, they must be able to transfer the concepts from one physical library to another. Even within a single library, specific resources and tools may change frequently as more information is purchased in an on-line format and as vendors continually improve and adapt their interfaces.

EDUCATIONAL CHANGE AND REFORM DEPENDS UPON INFORMATION LITERACY REQUIREMENTS

Students enabled and empowered by an information literacy requirement are prepared to take charge of their classroom experiences and to grapple with their disciplines rather than simply absorb information flowing from an instructor's mouth. When a campus accepts the Research Model as a priority, librarians need to be ready to plunge into restructuring efforts and to make strong arguments that students will not be able to meet the college's new goals and objectives without an information literacy requirement.

Already many campus communities are beginning to adopt learning-centered initiatives and programs. Evolving attitudes of faculty members and administrators about teaching and learning, made possible by educational change, provide opportunities for librarians to persuade the community that information literacy competence is an increasingly vital piece of students' college experience. By identifying core information competencies and documenting information literacy program options, librarians can partner in the process of transformation at its onset. Once this vision is embraced, a learning-centered approach to information literacy strategically relocates the learning library from the periphery of the campus to the heart of students' learning activities.

LIST OF LINKS

Information Literacy on the WWW
http://www.fiu.edu/~library/ili/iliweb.html

Information Literacy, IFL 101, York College of Pennsylvania
http://www.ycp.edu/library/ifl/etext/ethome.html

Catalyst
http://depts.washington.edu/catalyst/home.html

Information Literacy at Florida International University
http://www.fiu.edu/~library/ili/iliprop.html

Information Power, CLL373, Marylhurst College
http://www.marylhurst.edu/library/lib/win99syl.htm
http://www.marylhurst.edu/library/lib/infop.htm

Information Literacy: Critical Skills for a Changing World, LIS 1001,
Manhattanville College
http://www.mville.edu/library/LIS1001/lis1001.htm

Introduction to Library Research, LIB 101, Plattsburgh State University of New York
http://www.plattsburgh.edu/library/er/lib101sy.htm

UWired FIG Group Page
http://depts.washington.edu/nsp/fig/fig.html

ACRL Instruction Section Teaching Methods Committee's Examples
of Good Web-Based Library Tutorials
http://www.bk.psu.edu/academic/library/istm/tutorials.html

Information Literacy Program, California State University at San Marcos
http://ww2.csusm.edu/library/ILP/

QUICK BIB

Grassian, Esther and Susan E. Clark. "Information Literacy Sites." *C&RL News* 60, 2 (February 1999): 78-81, 92-93.

Kuhlthau, Carol Collier. "Developing a Model of the Library Search Process: Cognitive and Affective Aspects." *RQ* 28 (1998): 232-42.

_____ . "Learning in Digital Libraries: An Information Search Process Approach." *Library Trends* 45 (1997): 708-24.

McKinzie, Steve. "Research Across the Curriculum: Integrating Our Teaching with Our Institution's Academic Goals." In *Finding Common Ground: Creating the Library of the Future Without Diminishing the Library of the Past*, edited by Cheryl LaGuardia and Barbara A. Mitchell, 250-252. New York: Neal-Schuman Publishers, 1998.

NOTES

1. Patricia Iannuzzi at Florida International University maintains an excellent site, listing links to Web pages that analyze and describe competencies and standards (http://www.fiu.edu/~library/ili/iliweb.html).

2. The Research Model of education must be evident in all designs. For details on the theory of designing learning-centered information literacy instruction, the author recommends two articles by Kuhlthau, who has conducted extensive research about students' information-seeking behavior and has written detailed guides to applying a learning-centered approach to information literacy. In the article, "Learning in Digital Libraries: An Information Search Process Approach," Kuhlthau provides a picture of what librarians, students and faculty will actually do in the context of the information literacy requirement (Kuhlthau 1997). The "Model of the Search Process" identifies when and how students are most likely to welcome librarian intervention within a particular research project and provides guidance as campuses negotiate the logistics of their information literacy requirement (Kuhlthau 1998, 237).

REFERENCES

Campbell, Susan. E-mail interview. 28 October 1998.

Committee on Library User Education. "Rebooting the Library User Education Program @ UNO." *LLA Bulletin* 60, no. 3 (1998): 126-35.

Hoffmann, Gretchen McCord. "Library Instruction in Transition: Questioning Current Views." In *Finding Common Ground: Creating the Library of the Future Without Diminishing the Library of the Past,* edited by Cheryl LaGuardia and Barbara A. Mitchell, 144-151. New York: Neal-Schuman Publishers, 1998.

LaGuardia, Cheryl. *"Desk Set* Revisited: Reference Librarians, Reality, & Research Systems' Design." *Journal of Academic Librarianship* 21 (Jan. 1995): 7-9.

List, Carla. "Branching Out: A Required Library Research Course Targets Disciplines and Programs" *The Reference Librarian* 51-52 (1995): 385-98.

_____ . E-mail interview. 9 June 1998.

Orme, William A. "Librarians & Learning Communities." *BI-L* (10 Sept. 1998): n. pag. Online. 11 Sept. 1998.

Parise, Perina. E-mail interview. 10 June 1998.

Rubin, Susan. E-mail interview. 12 June 1998.

Saia, David. "Advocacy for Bibliographic Instruction: A Challenge for the Future," *The Katherine Sharp Review* 1 (Summer 1995): 34 pars. 12 Dec. 1998 <http://edfu.lis.uiuc.edu/review/summer1995/saia.pdf>.

Sonntag, Gabriela. E-mail interview. 23 June 1998.

From the Other Side of the River: Re-Conceptualizing the Educational Mission of Libraries

Barbara MacAdam

SUMMARY. Loyal to long-held convictions of what undergraduates need intellectually, academic librarians ignore the critical signs that they may be failing students and faculty. Unless librarians are willing to question assumptions about how students think, what they value, and how external incentives shape their behavior in the information environment, they will find themselves increasingly at the margins of students' academic life. If there are important questions that beg for answers before librarians can redefine the teaching role of libraries, librarians have probably never been in a stronger position as a profession to engage in the research necessary for meaningful solutions. *[Article copies available for a fee from The Haworth Document Delivery Service: 1-800-342-9678. E-mail address: getinfo@haworthpressinc.com <Website: http://www.haworthpress inc.com>]*

KEYWORDS. Library instruction, teaching library, college students, learning style, information literacy, critical thinking, digital libraries, networked information

Loyal to long-held convictions of what undergraduates need intellectually, academic librarians ignore the critical signs that they may be failing students and faculty. Without questioning assumptions about

Barbara MacAdam (AMLS, The University of Michigan) is Head of Educational and Information Services, University of Michigan Library, Ann Arbor, MI 48109-1185.

[Haworth co-indexing entry note]: "From the Other Side of the River: Re-Conceptualizing the Educational Mission of Libraries." MacAdam, Barbara. Co-published simultaneously in *College & Undergraduate Libraries* (The Haworth Press, Inc.) Vol. 6, No. 2, 2000, pp. 77-93; and: *Future Teaching Roles for Academic Librarians* (ed: Alice Harrison Bahr) The Haworth Press, Inc., 2000, pp. 77-93. Single or multiple copies of this article are available for a fee from The Haworth Document Delivery Service [1-800-342-9678, 9:00 a.m. - 5:00 p.m. (EST). E-mail address: getinfo@haworthpressinc.com].

how students think, what they value, and how external incentives shape their behavior in the information environment, librarians will find themselves increasingly at the margins of students' academic life.

FOOD FOR THOUGHT

Several years ago, the University of Michigan Library introduced a Core Journals project providing links from indexes in the on-line catalog to many periodical articles in full text. The following scenario ensued.

Week 1. Students become aware that they can request a print of some journal articles rather than hunt down a volume in the library and photocopy an item. The library is not charging for printing, and library printers are soon printing articles non-stop as student requests mount. Staff scurry to keep the volume of printed items under some control.

Week 2. Increasingly unwilling to track down printed materials, students prefer to use **only** on-line full-text articles. The volume of printed items continues to increase. Students print indiscriminately, leaving rejected articles behind. Piles of unclaimed rejects build up, and staff scurry to recycle them after forty-eight hours.

Week 3. Students become aware of the stacks of "rejects" building up around library printers and begin rooting through them directly for items on their topic. Appalled, staff redouble efforts in instruction, and at the reference desk, to guide students in appropriate research strategy.

Week 4. Staff explore mechanisms to charge for core journal printing. (Students authenticate with their campus network id and password when requesting a print of an article; the per page charges are logged against their campus computing fund allocations, with fund transfers back to the library.) When instituted some months later, the page-charge dramatically reduces the printing volume, and students appear to become far more selective in print requests.

This scenario should seem familiar. Although details vary, every academic professional has noticed some common elements in student behavior in the networked digital environment. Initial reactions are probably the same: shock, distress, and a reinforced view of student ignorance in the research process. As knowledge professionals, librarians **know** that students will never gather relevant and authoritative information on any topic based solely on instant availability. The goals of a liberal education include the willingness to engage in open-minded inquiry, shaped by the ability to think critically and synthesize logically and honestly. And although librarians may be amused, sympathetic, concerned, even galvanized to action by such dramatic evidence of student needs for information literacy, they **know** that they are right and students are wrong. This complacence is reinforced by frequently voiced faculty concerns about students' approach to intellectual activity.

Academic librarians are caught in a double bind. They take justifiable pride in the transformation of collections, services, and professional roles during the last decade. While this shift in roles may have begun as a necessary, and sometimes grudging, response to rapidly changing external events, librarians have become the leaders and catalysts on campuses for the digitization of knowledge and electronic access. Accordingly, they feel responsible for the environment in which students and faculty are trying to work. With decades of commitment as a profession to the instructional role of libraries, librarians further feel a special burden as educators for student success in information retrieval. They are vulnerable to implied criticism when a faculty member reports that her students relied solely on Internet sources, even after experiencing library instruction designed to educate and motivate them otherwise. In direct dealings with students, they are encouraged when students occasionally perceive that the ways they persist in doing things are not really "good" for them. "I got this information off the Web," a student may still say hopefully but sheepishly, anticipating a good-natured, but firm steer toward the "right stuff."

Librarians' knowledge base in instruction, emphasis on curriculum partnerships, and national leadership role in information literacy and digital libraries all conspire to hide the one question librarians should be asking. What if students are right and we are wrong? What if the instinctive way undergraduates do things is actually better suited than we think to successful work in the information environment of the future?

DISSECTING THE QUESTION

If librarians would examine long-held assumptions about student cognition, behavior, and affect, they might agree on the following set of principles.

- Undergraduates are still learning that most things are complex, most things cannot be known absolutely, most issues have two sides. Because they are still in intellectual transition, however, they want explicit answers and clear-cut processes (Perry, 1970).

- Undergraduates experience considerable anxiety doing research and using the library. They go through fairly predictable phases of affect during this process (Kuhlthau, 1994).
- Undergraduates are unfamiliar with the knowledge resources within disciplines, and with the way that specific disciplines generate information. They rarely understand the distinctions between popular and scholarly literature.
- Undergraduates underestimate the time needed for research and don't anticipate adequately the practical setbacks they may encounter. They often wait until the last minute to begin their library work, and have unrealistic expectations that work will somehow be already done for them.
- Undergraduates may know how to search the Web, but don't know how to evaluate Web resources critically. They lack the variety of skills and understanding to search various on-line systems in the academic library successfully.
- Undergraduates do not like to read, are impatient, have increasingly short attention spans, lack respect for authority and a reverence for the book-dependent culture at the heart of true knowledge and a full life (MacAdam, 1995).

Those assumptions have strongly influenced the traditional strategies academic librarians use to reshape undergraduate thinking and behavior. Typical instructional goals include helping students understand the need to gather multiple perspectives on an issue, to evaluate sources critically, to devise and execute a sound search strategy for a topic. Students are expected to recognize the need to allow adequate time for research, to develop a familiarity with the basic structure of information in a discipline, to know the difference between popular and scholarly literature. Librarians also want students to view the library as a welcoming place and to gain basic navigation skills in searching library catalogs, other on-line systems, and the Web.

The assumptions and strategies outlined above rest upon a standard "deficit model" approach, i.e., that undergraduates are somehow lacking, and need to have a compensating and corrective fix in thinking, feeling, and behavior before they will be able to use the library effectively. Librarians further believe that using the library effectively is tantamount to doing academic work successfully, and students are motivated to academic success. There is considerable logic to the deficit model. After all, students come to college lacking a knowledge base in organic chemistry, or social anthropology, or Northern Renaissance art. Students may also lack the a priori desire to learn these subjects. It is a natural extension that if the role of higher education is to develop a knowledge base in students that was not there before and to instill the desire and ability to learn independently, then the educational role of libraries should be the same.

But what if we de-couple for the moment the teaching role of libraries and the educational role of the academic curriculum? Much of the instruction done in academic library programs is based on the belief that the library's role is that of curriculum partner, in which the librarian and faculty member each supply an important, but not identical, intellectual component to the process. Academic librarians may find that they can build upon the skills of the new undergraduate in unexpected ways. It might be conceivable to consider an entirely new possibility: that while undergraduates still lack a knowledge of organic chemistry, they are already natural critical thinkers, savvy information consumers, and skilled information retrievers in ways faculty and librarians have yet to acknowledge. In short, what if all the thinking and behavior students exhibit is not *wrong* for this information environment, but precisely the conceptualization and skills now required?

THE STUDENT AS TEACHER

Return for a moment to the original scenario of student "misuse" of the full-text journal service. It was characterized as wrong because

- the student is overlooking or ignoring what may be the most appropriate or relevant material
- the student is completing a paper or assignment based on incomplete information or information that may be in error; the quality of the completed assignment will therefore be significantly compromised
- the student is losing what may be the most important intellectual aspects of the assignment–the careful framing of the topic or information need, and the systematic rigor of information gathering and synthesis at the heart of scholarly inquiry.

- By reducing the process to a thoughtless grab off the information market shelves, the student relinquishes all the potential to develop as an information literate, critical thinker likely to be more successful in later life.

Why not look at this purely through an undergraduate's eyes? To do this successfully requires setting aside personal and traditional value judgments.

I am a nineteen year old student who has a paper to write. There are a lot of demands on my time: part-time job, class reading to catch up on, calculus homework, mid-terms in two weeks, and an every-day life where each experience or connection with people is unbelievably engaging. I do not give the library a moment's thought, except when I absolutely have to go there to get something done related to class. I find I can spend fifteen minutes at a computer workstation, somehow bring up some citations that appear to be about U.S. economic policy toward China, and get a few printed out on a printer several feet away. There will probably be a "keeper" or two which I'll be able to tell better once I've got them in hand, and I'll leave the rest behind. I also found some sites on the Web that look pretty useful. I manage to pull together a paper from the material that I've retrieved, things I've picked up from my text, or maybe the faculty member's comments. I'm not the world's greatest writer, but I generally do OK, so I spend five or six hours at a computing lab writing my paper. I turn it in and get a B+. I'm pretty pleased with that (and for my first college paper, my parents likely will be, too). I'll probably do even better next time, because I'm picking up new things all the time.

That scenario is exaggerated, but forces the essential question. Doesn't this particular student's perception and consequent behavior seem logical? Don't the "right" alternatives a librarian would urge begin to appear ludicrous? Consider what instruction librarians say to students. Frame your topic carefully and narrow it appropriately; map out a search strategy; consider some background material; decide if you need a scholarly perspective, or data, or interpretation in the mass media. Evaluate each source carefully; consider the relation to each other; make sure you get balanced points of view. Most scholarly literature is still in print format, so allow time to gather your material, and try not to get frustrated that things are checked out, off the shelf, or not owned by the library.

Keep in mind what your life is like as a student. You might book an airline reservation on-line, or at least by phone, and put it on a credit card. Last semester you may have even bought a textbook or your favorite CD from Amazon.com. You still follow the Philadelphia Flyers minute by minute on the NHL site–in fact your screen saver has a freeze frame you downloaded from the last highlight clip on the site. Between Net, phone, fax, e-mail, your sense of being able to work seven days a week, twenty-four hours a day, and engage with much of the rest of the world is reinforced in every facet of your life. Your college just began keeping the computer labs open twenty-four hours/ day, and your residence hall has an Ethernet jack in every room. Whenever you go on the Web with a search, you always find at least something, and the time flies by. Your time matters to you, and you are outcome oriented, so you measure success by the result, not by a separately constructed set of values.

And what if you are **not** this student, but come to college as one of the information have nots? Your overall perception of the world constructed along the lines above has been solidly implanted by the mass media, although your actual exposure to information technology through family, schools, and peer group may be far more limited. Your very lack of technology skills, combined with your institutional emphasis on seeing that you acquire them, is likely to leave you with greater frustration and impatience with processes that appear confusing, unproductive, and outmoded.

If you can, even for a brief moment, **feel** this through the psyche of a student, then you will get it. And you cannot begin to consider the implications for academic libraries unless you get it.

TRYING TO PUT NEW WINE IN OLD BOTTLES

Academic librarians understand how profoundly the information environment has changed during recent years. The problem comes in the failure to reexamine the instructional strategies of the past with a critical enough eye. Let me begin by suggesting some heretical views of this recent past, not because past strategies didn't work, but precisely because their effectiveness makes them so hard to relinquish now.

SEARCH STRATEGY

Instruction librarians have concentrated on helping students develop a conceptual understanding of a research process appropriate to the need at hand. This process, if followed reasonably, should lead to a successful outcome. Success might be defined as focused, balanced, accurate, and complete information relevant to the subject, suitable for academic inquiry, and with enough relation among the content to permit a realistic synthesis for a five-page paper (or twenty-page paper). Science, social sciences, arts and humanities, with different structures to their component disciplines called for variant search strategies. The process was predominantly linear, logical, systematic, and consciously analytical.

The fact that scholars in any field did not work like this was irrelevant (Perrow, 1989). Faculty **knew** the subject matter. Undergraduates required a systematic process because their limited knowledge permitted no short cuts, e.g., contacting an expert colleague. Information gathering also required the systematic **physical** gathering of material, so, in spite of a somewhat artificial search strategy, there was a natural harmony between intellectual linearity and the tangible collation of print content.

INFORMATION RETRIEVAL SKILLS

Hands-on, skill-based information retrieval instruction has been a key, and highly necessary, requirement of the structured world of formal information, coupled with the command-driven, on-line catalog. So, too, has been understanding controlled vocabulary as a concept mapped uniquely to subject search terms and the explicit rules for entry in any system. Lack of understanding and mistakes did not result in just poor information, but no information. Judgment was swift and inexorable, and the incentive to learn rules was adequate for student, faculty, and librarian alike. There was a comforting veneer of precision to the whole process, and the degrees of freedom were limited.

EVALUATION AND CRITICAL THINKING

There were obvious distinctions between *TV Guide* and the *Columbia Journalism Review,* between a book and journal article, a government document and a letter to the editor in a newspaper. The concept of an author might occasionally be complicated, but answering "who wrote this" was generally less challenging than the more substantive question of what biases or perspectives that author might bring. Undergraduates may have been equally content with the first information available, but could make distinctions readily once acquainted with the difference among formats and authority of sources. Since such information presented itself in predictable garb, librarians could point out the distinctions, and faculty could easily reinforce for "good" content and provide disincentives for "bad." It was fair enough–there were rules that could be communicated, and sanctions implied: "Don't use popular magazines," warned the faculty member. "Don't use *Readers' Guide*," admonished the librarian. Following the rules might not guarantee a good paper, but could prevent disaster in the bibliography domain.

WARM AND FUZZY

Students were intimidated by academic libraries, and anxious about the search process. Encouraging them to ask questions, to feel confident that someone would help them, that their ignorance was in fact understandable and even welcome, were all part of instruction. The information environment was the natural home of scholars and librarians, not hapless 18-year-olds. It took effort to minimize this dissonance and make a challenging environment more accessible.

In summary, the thought process, behavior, and emotion of ordinary life had to be recast for students to be successful in academic libraries. Life was natural, libraries were human-constructed artifices. So librarians taught students things, to shield them from the errors they would inevitably make by following their natural inclinations. And this is what they continue to try and do.

PROPOSING A NEW SET OF ASSUMPTIONS

- Raised on the steady diet of mass media and advertising, undergraduates tend to be cynical and are willing to challenge authority. They are naturally critical, even iconoclastic in their thinking.
- Students are naturally democratic and will give most new ideas a fair shot, but will move quickly and decisively to judgment.
- Undergraduates have a rich intellectual and emotional life. They are comfortable and practiced in argument, and the value of polite discussion for its own sake eludes them.
- From Internet chat rooms to their sojourn in K-12 curriculum, they like to collaborate with others. They gravitate naturally to

situations where they can be active participants, with a certain energy and sense of fun.

- Bombarded with constant graphic and information stimuli, they expect the unexpected. The predictable, systematic and orderly appears unrealistic and unnatural to them.
- Teaching faculty may complain about student study and work habits, but students in the main appear to find ways to complete their academic work successfully on their own.
- Grounded in a market economy and surrounded by rampant consumerism, students are used to being courted in highly competitive fashion for their time, attention, and money. They are not likely to lower their standards for service when they enter a library.
- Librarians and other academics experience considerable anxiety and frustration in the current information environment, students do not.
- Undergraduates are emotionally and intellectually at home in the digital, networked information environment. In fact they are shaping that environment with an influence and power unprecedented for the young intellect (Tapscott, 1998).

If academic librarians are willing to accept at least some of these assumptions, then it may be clearer why there is such a natural mesh between today's information environment and undergraduates. It will also help librarians understand why they need to re-conceptualize their vision of a teaching library.

SEARCH STRATEGY REPRISE

The sheer volume of content in the networked environment lends itself to picking up discernible patterns and following common threads of meaning across content. Contrary opinions tend to converge upon an idea quickly on the Internet. Rather than trying to teach a formal and linear search strategy, accept a new "signal to noise" model that assumes that a "successful" search query will pull up the worthless side by side with the valuable. The saving grace is that it does so with enough speed that the time can be devoted to the view and discard stage, rather than the retrieval stage. With the proliferation of full text, there's a better basis for making a judgment, thus evening the odds for the critical acumen of the younger intellect. The end result will not necessarily turn out to be poorer, provided undergraduates understand that each click of the mouse represents a selective choice among content.

BEING CRITICAL ABOUT CRITICAL THINKING

Remember that students are naturally critical in everyday life. Trying to get them to follow a set of web site evaluation criteria consciously as they fly from URL to URL is unrealistic. Worse, it is precisely contrary to the nature of the Web, and how humans work within it. It may be time to set aside worries that they'll never find the right, the best, or even good information, and just use instructional interventions to tell them, "Trust your instincts." The more time they spend engaging with the Web, the better their instincts will be in general.

Above all, librarians need to keep in mind that the vast majority of undergraduate academic life always has been, and should be, spent engaging with a subject itself. Lectures, discussion, readings, assignments, lab work, all expand students' intellectual grasp and build contextual instincts for information. Before we persist in arguing that students cannot develop such contextual instincts without librarian intervention, accept this reality: Students routinely produce decent papers and assignments without a librarian at their side. That doesn't marginalize a librarian's role, it just means that there are many critical dimensions to successful academic work. **The single most important step academic librarians can take right now is to help faculty find ways to develop curriculum bridges from the natural critical nature of students to the formal contextual judgments they must make in any specific subject discipline.**

DO GOOD COLLECTIONS ALWAYS FINISH LAST?

It is an interesting and provocative phenomenon that academic librarians often appear to assume that students' inexperience will invariably lead them to the worst information and keep them from finding the best. Pure chance should lead undergraduates to carefully assembled and organized library digital resources at least 50 percent of the time even if they try to avoid anything in print.

Librarians are onto something in perceiving that students would rather do an Internet search than wrestle with more complex knowl-

edge systems now in direct competition with so many other information resources. The immediate reaction is to attribute this equally to
undergraduate disinclination for serious work and to the failure of
instruction to develop students' critical judgment. But unless librarians believe that faculty are fully conversant with the electronic environment librarians have created, it is probably time to accept that
librarians haven't made intuitive search systems and clearly organized
digital content their highest priority.

THE TEACHING LIBRARY AS A SERVICE ORGANIZATION

Students are a neglected part of service focus, even in college and
undergraduate libraries ostensibly focused on their needs. Librarians
try to make sure the photocopiers are working, the environment is
welcoming, and the building is open long hours. They carefully select
digital resources for the virtual reference collection and still make sure
that collections include the books needed for the undergraduate curriculum. They devote themselves heart and soul to instruction and reference, and are dedicated to their role as educational partners.

What librarians may not see is that their educational goals are
sometimes in conflict with their service goals. Part of being a teacher
is to guide a student through a learning process, so that intellectual and
character growth can take place. A certain dimension of struggle, of
frustration, of success, and occasional failure, is part of this growth.
Think about the academic grading structure that builds in a value
system where some endeavors *must* be less successful than others in
order to define accomplishment. There is a lurking sentiment among
all academic librarians that a certain amount of slogging is good for
the undergraduate soul, that it correlates with the self-discipline and
commitment requisite for acquiring knowledge of substance, as well
as the ethos of the life-long learner.

Librarians think of instantaneous and distance-independent document delivery, for example, as a service goal for faculty, and information on a platter as the modus operandi of the special librarian because
faculty and professionals demand and deserve such client-centered
service. But when students behave like faculty, placing a premium on
their time, demonstrating high value for prompt and accurate information, and displaying the clear ability to make conscious and logical
cost/benefit choices, we consider this wrong. Recall the anecdote

about the full-text journals project, and look at it through a different lens. Students were making an astute choice that quick, simple, and free access to content trumped slow, hard, and cost-laden information any day. They made another logical choice in modulating their preferences when confronted with a new cost model. This isn't immature, lazy, or ignorant behavior, it is eminently "professional."

Students have high expectations of everything: from the look and value of Web sites, to the ease and functionality of systems, and the speed and cost of services. Libraries persisting in making students do things the "hard" way because it is good for them don't look like educational partners, they look like poor libraries, and not very good value for student tuition dollars. Libraries had their rules and stuck to them. Students had no choice but to live within them, and there was no Amazon.com to provoke their higher expectations. It is time to re-scrutinize services from a student viewpoint and stop mixing up the many practical elements of information gathering, in both the print and digital or virtual environment, with the work of the intellect. By reducing the efforts students devote to the former, librarians can protect their time and focus for the latter.

What students want and need from a reference desk in terms of user-centered service often differs surprisingly little from faculty (Massey-Burzio, 1998). But before librarians can apply available research to the design of relevant and effective services, they need to set aside pejorative views that serve as barriers to open discussion about reference:

- They only want us to do their work **for** them.
- Expecting everything to be digital or accessible electronically is just a mark of student ignorance.
- If they cared about a subject or about learning, they would be willing to put in the time and thought research requires.

Instead, try to see the student view of the world as a service goal libraries are ultimately working toward. Librarians may perceive faculty as the primary audience for ease of scholarly knowledge access, but can surely appreciate the benefits to students.

As a possible blueprint for service, consider the following:

- Provide reference service that avoids making students jump through a set of hoops that would never be demanded of faculty.

Use the reference setting as a prime opportunity for the "learning moment." Continually challenge the assumption that making students do something the hard way is inherently good for them and part of the educational process.

- Finite resources and views toward students conspire to make academic librarians justify withholding from students the services they make available (or wish they could) to faculty. If a faculty member finds a pull-and-copy or other document-delivery service convenient, why wouldn't students, who find the library harder to use and who work under even shorter deadlines, find them even more so? Every library must make choices in priorities for what services it can realistically provide to segments of its user community. However, librarians should take students' desire for gold-standard service as a sign of their sophistication, maturity, and common sense, not just self indulgence.

- Hold any new system up to tougher standards. If it takes staff a two-hour introductory session and a two hour advanced session to become familiar with a resource, think about the implications for students. And if it is remotely possible to deploy an existing system in a way that an intelligent student can use it, make the commitment to devote staff resources to the necessary design and implementation. If designing a web site, there is no excuse for poor functionality or design, and if acquiring a necessary information resource for a research environment, then be willing to put aside unrealistic expectations of the independent user.

- Make instruction a learner-centered endeavor. How often have you heard reference staff bemoan: "Why don't all students have to take a class in using the on-line catalog?" or "Students don't pay attention in class and then expect us to teach them the basics every time they come to the desk!" It is time to set aside expectations of when and how students **should** learn, and how they **do** learn. Why are librarians so unwilling to reframe observed behavior, which is assumed a sign that instruction has "failed" rather than for what it is?

Undergraduate behavior should be viewed as ongoing user input signaling more loudly than any survey or focus group, "Pay attention! This is what I need to learn, and this is exactly how, and when, I want to learn it." Students aren't unwilling to learn what we're trying to teach them, the who, what, when, where, and why is just still wrong far too often. The fact that faculty continue to request course-integrated instruction in ever-growing numbers doesn't automatically validate actual learning outcome for the student. Perhaps librarians' instincts are more accurate in questioning the amount of effort balanced against the observable gains.

Academic librarians are not wrong to explore self-paced, technology-based instruction, or any other innovations to teach students, but they should make greater use of the obvious opportunities and devote themselves to a professional culture change. The professional literature on active learning is probably more relevant to today's students than ever. Librarians should, in fact, revisit their instructional foundations, encouraged by the possibility that the knowledge environment has both produced, and been produced by, our future undergraduates. These students may be more suited than ever to work with each other, and with us, in incredibly productive ways.

REDEFINING THE TEACHING ROLE OF LIBRARIANS

If academic librarians were to create a road map to guide their undergraduate teaching role during the next few years, they should focus on the following priorities:

- Identify and take advantage of any possible opportunity to work with teaching faculty to help them understand how students really think and work in the contemporary information environment.
- Collaborate with faculty in the design of curriculum and assignments that integrate information gathering and synthesis intellectually within a disciplinary context.
- Develop a systematic and ongoing way to evaluate how undergraduates think and use digital knowledge resources and networked information systems, and incorporate those findings quickly and effectively back into system and service design.
- Reemphasize reference as a context-specific, learner-centered teaching opportunity, even if it comes at the expense of traditional library instruction.
- Participate in **all** campus initiatives designed to improve, support, and expand undergraduate education: academic and student support program development, new facility design, accreditation standards, cultural enrichment, recruiting and retention efforts,

faculty adoption of instructional technology, and development of information technology infrastructure and policy.

THE OTHER SIDE OF THE RIVER

The problem with a new perspective is that it inevitably means letting go of what came before. In the rush to do so, there is a risk of forgetting that not everything examined is found wanting. If librarians return to the goals of a liberal education, and to the intrinsic values of higher education, they have relinquished nothing. Students are confronting the world less through books, but they engage with it very directly in equally powerful ways. Their curiosity, willingness to investigate, read, write, devote themselves to ideas, talk, and collaborate isn't less, it is probably greater than ever. For many decades, academic librarians have devoted much of their intellectual, emotional, and operational effort to making students feel comfortable and helping them work effectively in libraries. Some of those specifics can be jettisoned, if they can see the way more clearly. Initiatives such as the Association of College and Research Libraries' Institute for Information Literacy, intended to train instruction librarians and to develop programming for library administrators on information issues, have the potential to help a new generation of librarians understand what students need and how to teach them effectively.

Academic librarians are at the forefront of digital resource creation and the design of systems to access this knowledge. Faculty, who themselves struggle anew with technology and the need to develop fresh relationships with their undergraduates, will benefit immeasurably from librarians' insights. Librarians, after all, see students more immediately as they go about their academic work. Librarians simply need to collaborate more substantively with faculty toward a shared vision of how the undergraduate's way of working relates to the intellectual growth faculty and librarians want from students.

Finally, let me suggest another way to look at the debate surrounding the dramatic changes in professional education during the last few years. A much broader range of scholarship and breadth of professional practice now serves as the foundation of academic librarianship. If there are important questions that beg for answers before librarians can redefine the teaching role of libraries, they have probably never been in a stronger position as a profession to engage in the research necessary for meaningful solutions.

REFERENCES

Kaulthau, Carol. *Teaching the Library Research Process*, 2d ed. New York: Scarecrow Press, 1994.

MacAdam, Barbara. "Sustaining the Culture of the Book: The Role of Enrichment Reading and Critical Thinking in the Undergraduate Curriculum." *Library Trends* 44 (Fall 1995): 238-263.

Massey-Burzio, Virginia. "From the Other Side of the Reference Desk: A Focus Group." *The Journal of Academic Librarianship* 24 (May 1998): 208-215.

Perrow, Charles. "On Not Using Libraries." In *Humanists At Work: Disciplinary Perspectives and Personal Reflections*. Proceedings of Symposium Sponsored by the Institute for the Humanities and the University Library, The University of Illinois at Chicago. Chicago, Illinois: April 27-28, 1989, 29-42.

Perry, William Graves. *Forms of Intellectual and Ethical Development In the College Years*. New York: Holt, Rinehart, and Winston, 1978.

Tapscott, Don. *Growing Up Digital: The Rise of the Net Generation*. New York: McGraw Hill, 1998.

Index